Haunted by the Jersey Devil: A Journey into American Folklore

Oliver Lancaster

Published by Oliver Lancaster, 2023.

While every precaution has been taken in the preparation of this book, the publisher assumes no responsibility for errors or omissions, or for damages resulting from the use of the information contained herein.

HAUNTED BY THE JERSEY DEVIL: A JOURNEY INTO AMERICAN FOLKLORE

First edition. July 31, 2023.

Copyright © 2023 Oliver Lancaster.

ISBN: 979-8223288992

Written by Oliver Lancaster.

Also by Oliver Lancaster

Chernobyl: Unveiling the tragedy. A Comprehensive Account of the Nuclear Disaster

The Bhopal Gas Tragedy: Unraveling the Catastrophe of 1984

The Deepwater Horizon Oil Spill of 2010: A Disaster Unveiled

Fukushima Fallout: Unveiling the Truth behind the 2011 Nuclear Disaster

Minamata Disease: Poisoned Waters and the Battle for Justice (1932-1968)

Evil Women: Unmasking History's Most Notorious Women

Bundy The Dark Chronicles: America's Infamous Serial Killer

Dahmer The Dark Chronicles: America's Infamous Milwaukee Cannibal

Zodiac The Dark Chronicles: America's Infamous Cryptic Killer

Bigfoot: The Comprehensive Investigation into the Elusive Legend

Chasing Legends: The Truth behind the Chupacabra

Chasing Legends: The Truth behind the Loch Ness Monster

Aokigahara Forest: The Heartbreaking Secrets of Japan's Suicide Forest

The Amityville House: The Haunting Secrets of America's Most Infamous Residence

The Stanley Hotel: The Mystery of Colorado's Historic Landmark

The Tower of London: The Haunted Past and Secrets of Royal Ghosts

The Winchester Mystery House: The Riddle of Sarah Winchester's Mansion

Vanished Skies: The Mysterious Disappearance of Amelia Earhart

Vanishing Point: The Bermuda Triangle Exposed

Poveglia Island: Haunting Secrets of Italy's Most Terrifying Haunted Destination

Tracing Footsteps: The Mystery of Madeleine McCann

Inferno in the Sky: The Hindenburg Disaster

Challenger: Tragedy and Triumph - Unraveling the Space Shuttle Challenger Explosion

Collision Course: Unraveling The Tenerife Airport Disaster

Haunted by the Jersey Devil: A Journey into American Folklore

Sweet Tragedy: Unraveling The Boston Molasses Disaster

Watch for more at https://tinyurl.com/olanc.

Sign up to my free newsletter to get updates on new releases, FREE teaser chapters to upcoming releases and FREE digital short stories.

Or visit https://tinyurl.com/olanc

I never spam and you can unsubscribe at any time.

OLIVER LANCASTER

Disclaimer

This book is a work of non-fiction based on research and historical accounts. While we strive for accuracy, the content presents interpretations of folklore and paranormal investigations. The subject matter involves mythical creatures, and readers' perceptions may vary. Any resemblance to actual events or persons, living or dead, is coincidental.

Haunted by the Jersey Devil: A Journey into American Folklore

INTRODUCTION

Chapter 1: The Legend Takes Flight

Chapter 2: Folktales and Local Beliefs

Chapter 3: Historical Context and Cultural Impact

Chapter 4: Cryptozoology and Scientific Perspectives

Chapter 5: Historical Sightings and Unexplained Incidents

Chapter 6: Legends from the Pines

Chapter 7: Hoaxes and Pranks

Chapter 8: Legends of Abductions and Mysterious Disappearances

Chapter 9: Exploring Paranormal Explanations

Chapter 10: The Jersey Devil in Modern Culture

Chapter 11: Psychological and Sociological Aspects

Chapter 12: Cryptids and Cryptotourism

Chapter 13: Theories of Origin

Chapter 14: The Search for Physical Evidence

Chapter 15: Cryptozoology and Conservation

Chapter 16: Skeptics and Debunkers

Chapter 17: The Legacy of the Jersey Devil

HAUNTED BY THE JERSEY DEVIL: A JOURNEY INTO AMERICAN FOLKLORE

Conclusion

OLIVER LANCASTER

Introduction

The legend of the Jersey Devil has been an enduring and enigmatic part of American folklore for centuries, captivating the imaginations of people from all walks of life. Nestled deep within the pine barrens of southern New Jersey, this mythical creature has left an indelible mark on the region's culture and history. From frightening encounters in the dark woods to eerie sightings on stormy nights, the legend of the Jersey Devil has grown and evolved over time, becoming a prominent aspect of American storytelling.

The origins of the Jersey Devil date back to the early 18th century, making it one of the oldest and most persistent folktales in the United States. The tale is deeply ingrained in the cultural fabric of the region, transcending generations and maintaining its relevance even in the modern world. It has inspired numerous books, movies, and artworks, solidifying its place as a cultural icon and a symbol of mystery and fear.

The Jersey Devil is said to have been born as the cursed thirteenth child of Mother Leeds, a woman who lived in the Pine Barrens during the colonial era. According to the legend, she was already burdened by her many children and cried out, "Let this one be the Devil!" during the birth, unknowingly invoking a malevolent force. The child was born with the appearance of a monstrous creature: a grotesque mix of human and animal features. The Devil, after a brief time among humans, is said to have retreated to the vast wilderness of the Pine Barrens, where it has remained elusive and haunting ever since.

This folklore has seeped into the collective consciousness of the American people, becoming a fixture in local customs, storytelling, and even tourism. Visitors to the Pine Barrens seek out eerie experiences, hoping to catch a glimpse of the mythical creature. Countless tales of the Devil's encounters have been shared over campfires and in hushed whispers, reinforcing its place as a key figure in American folklore.

Moreover, the legend of the Jersey Devil has proven to be adaptable, expanding beyond its regional roots to resonate with people across the country. It has become a powerful symbol of the unknown and the supernatural, speaking to the human fascination with the mysterious and the unexplained. As a result, the Devil has found its way into literature, television shows, and various forms of popular culture, further solidifying its status as a timeless legend.

This book, "Haunted by the Jersey Devil: A Journey into American Folklore," seeks to delve deep into the heart of this extraordinary tale, uncovering the historical context, the various iterations of the legend, and the impact it has had on the people who have lived in its shadow. By exploring the origins, evolution, and significance of this iconic myth, we aim to shed light on how folklore shapes our understanding of the world, connecting us to our past and inviting us to ponder the mysteries that still lie beyond our comprehension. So, join us as we embark on a journey into the dark and fascinating realm of the Jersey Devil, where fact and fiction entwine, and the legend lives on.

The purpose of "Haunted by the Jersey Devil: A Journey into American Folklore" is to comprehensively explore the multifaceted legend of the Jersey Devil, dissecting its origins, tracing its historical context, and delving into the numerous theories that have emerged over the years. This book seeks to offer readers a comprehensive and informative guide that goes beyond mere retelling of the legend, providing a nuanced and in-depth analysis of its significance in American folklore.

1. Unraveling the Origins:

The book begins by delving into the origins of the Jersey Devil legend, tracing its roots back to the early 18th century and examining the tale's earliest iterations. It investigates the story of Mother Leeds, the supposed progenitor of the Devil, and explores the socio-cultural context of colonial America that may have contributed to the legend's creation. Drawing upon historical records, local accounts, and folkloric studies, the book aims to shed light on how the legend emerged and took root in the imagination of the people.

2. Historical Significance:

Moving forward, the book delves into the historical significance of the Jersey Devil in the context of American folklore. It explores how the tale of this enigmatic creature has persisted through the centuries, molding and adapting to the changing times. Readers will discover how the legend has been intertwined with regional identity and shaped the cultural heritage of southern New Jersey. By examining how the story of the Devil has been passed down through generations, the book aims to illustrate its lasting impact on the local community and its place in the broader spectrum of American folklore.

3. Folklore Evolution:

As folklore often evolves and takes on new dimensions, this book seeks to document the various iterations of the Jersey Devil legend over time. From oral tradition to written accounts and artistic representations, the Devil's story has experienced transformations and adaptations that have enriched its narrative. The book will explore how the legend has been retold, reshaped, and disseminated through different media, such as literature, visual arts, and mass media, reflecting changes in society's beliefs and fears.

4. Investigating Sightings and Encounters:

No exploration of the Jersey Devil would be complete without an examination of reported sightings and encounters. The book will delve into eyewitness accounts and alleged encounters with the mythical creature, presenting a diverse range of perspectives and evaluating the credibility of these claims. It will also analyze the psychological and sociological aspects behind the phenomenon of mass sightings, showing how belief in the Devil persists in the face of rational skepticism.

5. Theories and Explanations:

HAUNTED BY THE JERSEY DEVIL: A JOURNEY INTO AMERICAN FOLKLORE

While the Jersey Devil may be firmly rooted in folklore, numerous theories and explanations have been put forth to account for the legend's origins. This book aims to present these various hypotheses and evaluate their plausibility, ranging from historical events and misidentified animals to psychological and sociological factors. By exploring these theories, the book invites readers to consider the complex interplay between myth, reality, and human perception.

Overall, "Haunted by the Jersey Devil: A Journey into American Folklore" seeks to provide readers with a comprehensive, well-researched, and engaging exploration of this captivating legend. By combining historical analysis, folkloric research, and critical examination, the book aims to enrich readers' understanding of how folklore shapes cultural identity, perpetuates fears, and weaves a tapestry of myths that endure through the ages.

As the author of "Haunted by the Jersey Devil: A Journey into American Folklore," my personal fascination with this mythical creature has been a driving force behind this research and writing endeavor. Growing up in the United States, I was no stranger to local legends and ghost stories, but it was the tale of the Jersey Devil that truly captivated my imagination from a young age.

The first time I heard about the Jersey Devil was during a family camping trip to the Pine Barrens of New Jersey. Gathered around the campfire, surrounded by the vast darkness of the woods, an elder from the area regaled us with spine-chilling tales of the Devil's haunting presence. The vivid descriptions of its eerie appearance and the way it roamed the wilderness left a lasting impression on my young mind.

As I grew older, my curiosity about folklore and legends deepened, and I found myself drawn to stories that had stood the test of time, like that of the Jersey Devil. The enigmatic nature of the legend, coupled with the fact that it had been passed down for centuries, intrigued me immensely. What started as a childhood fascination evolved into a profound desire to understand the historical and cultural significance of this iconic creature in American folklore.

My journey in researching the Jersey Devil began with an exploration of local libraries, archives, and historical records. I immersed myself in dusty tomes and centuries-old newspaper clippings, unearthing the earliest accounts of the legend and uncovering the socio-cultural backdrop against which it emerged. The more I delved into its origins, the more I realized that this tale was not merely a figment of imagination but a reflection of the fears, beliefs, and historical context of its time.

Throughout the research process, I encountered an abundance of folklore experts, historians, and local residents who graciously shared their knowledge and experiences with the legend. Their willingness to share their stories, whether rooted in belief or skepticism, added layers of depth to my understanding of the Jersey Devil's enduring impact on the community.

While investigating the various theories and explanations surrounding the Jersey Devil, I found myself exploring a diverse range of disciplines, from biology and zoology to psychology and sociology. Each perspective offered unique insights into the ways that folklore can emerge from a confluence of factors, including misperceptions, ecological influences, and the human psyche's propensity for storytelling.

The most memorable part of my research journey was undoubtedly the fieldwork. Venturing into the Pine Barrens itself, I experienced firsthand the haunting beauty of this untamed wilderness. I spoke with locals who had grown up with stories of the Devil, their words carrying a mix of awe, fear, and a deep-rooted connection to their cultural heritage. While I may not have encountered the legendary creature during my travels, the encounters and conversations with people who believed they had made the folklore come alive in a tangible and visceral way.

Throughout this journey, my fascination with the Jersey Devil only deepened. The creature's elusiveness and its profound impact on the collective imagination of a community piqued my curiosity even further. This book is a culmination of my efforts to share the multifaceted nature of the legend, offering readers a chance to embark on their own journey into the world of American folklore, one filled with mystery, wonder, and the enduring power of storytelling.

Chapter 1: The Legend Takes Flight

The earliest accounts and origins of the Jersey Devil legend can be traced back to the 18th century, in the midst of the colonial era in America. The story centers around the Leeds family, who were prominent in the Pine Barrens of southern New Jersey. The most popular version of the tale revolves around Mother Leeds, a woman who was already burdened with twelve children and, upon learning she was pregnant with her thirteenth, reportedly exclaimed in frustration, "Let this one be the Devil!"

According to the legend, Mother Leeds' words were taken quite literally, and when she gave birth to her thirteenth child in 1735, the baby was born with deformities and grotesque features. The child's appearance was described as having wings, hooves, and a forked tail, reminiscent of a devil or mythical creature. The baby is said to have promptly transformed into a monstrous creature and fled into the night, disappearing into the Pine Barrens, where it has allegedly roamed ever since.

The Leeds family, who were already known for their eccentricities, became associated with the legend, and their name became synonymous with the creature. Over time, the tale spread throughout the region through oral tradition and storytelling, becoming an integral part of the local folklore. Various communities within the Pine Barrens began to claim sighting of the creature, solidifying its presence in the collective consciousness.

As with many legends, the story of the Jersey Devil evolved over time, taking on new details and variations. While the Leeds family's 13th child is the most widely known version, there are other accounts that suggest alternative origins. Some claim that the Devil was the result of a curse placed upon the Leeds family by a disgruntled witch or a Native American shaman. Others attribute the creature's creation to supernatural forces or demonic intervention.

One notable early written reference to the Jersey Devil can be found in a Leeds Point, New Jersey, resident's diary dating back to the 19th century. Joseph Bonaparte, the brother of Napoleon Bonaparte and a former resident of New Jersey, also reportedly claimed to have witnessed the Devil during his time in the region. These accounts added to the legend's notoriety and contributed to its enduring presence in American folklore.

While the origins of the Jersey Devil legend remain shrouded in mystery, scholars and folklorists have suggested several potential explanations. Some speculate that the story of the Devil may have been influenced by European folktales and superstitions brought over by the early settlers. Others propose that the legend could be an allegory for the harsh and untamed nature of the Pine Barrens, a region known for its dense forests, isolated communities, and challenging living conditions.

The Jersey Devil legend has proven to be remarkably resilient, transcending generations and adapting to changing times. It has become a prominent aspect of New Jersey's cultural identity and continues to intrigue and captivate people from all walks of life. Whether rooted in historical events, superstition, or a combination of both, the tale of the Jersey Devil has left an indelible mark on American folklore, perpetuating the fascination with the mysterious and unexplained.

The evolution of the Jersey Devil legend over time is a testament to the power of storytelling and its ability to adapt to changing contexts and incorporate local folklore and historical events. As the tale of the Devil was passed down through generations, it underwent various transformations, assimilating elements from different cultural influences, historical events, and local beliefs. This complex evolution has contributed to the legend's enduring appeal and its status as a cornerstone of American folklore.

The Jersey Devil legend emerged in the Pine Barrens region of New Jersey, a place shrouded in its own rich folklore and cultural heritage. As the tale spread within this isolated and tightly-knit community, it absorbed elements of existing local folklore, such as tales of other supernatural beings, mythical creatures, and ghostly apparitions that had long been a part of the area's oral tradition. By incorporating these elements, the legend of the Jersey Devil became deeply intertwined with the region's cultural identity, resonating with the fears, hopes, and beliefs of its inhabitants.

Historical events also played a role in shaping the legend of the Jersey Devil. The colonial era, during which the tale first emerged, was marked by a deeply religious society, and superstitions surrounding witchcraft and the supernatural were prevalent. The harsh living conditions in the Pine Barrens, with its dense forests and limited resources, likely contributed to the development of folktales as a form of entertainment and coping mechanism. Moreover, the Leeds family, whose name became linked to the Devil, were well-known in the region, further solidifying the story's local roots.

New Jersey's early settlers brought with them a rich tapestry of European folklore, which inevitably influenced the development of the Jersey Devil legend. The motif of a cursed or monstrous child, like that of Mother Leeds' thirteenth child, can be found in various European folktales. Elements of these stories merged with local folklore to give the Jersey Devil its distinctive characteristics, such as its devilish appearance and the idea of it being born from a human mother.

As the legend gained notoriety, especially in the 19th and 20th centuries, it attracted attention from the media, newspapers, and sensationalist publications. Reports of sightings and encounters were often exaggerated and sensationalized to capture public interest, further perpetuating the legend's mystique and allure. This media attention solidified the Devil's place in American popular culture and ensured its continued prominence in the public consciousness.

With the advent of technology and mass media, the legend of the Jersey Devil underwent further adaptation to suit contemporary tastes. It found its way into various forms of entertainment, including literature, movies, and television shows, each iteration offering new interpretations of the creature and its origins. This continuous reinvention has allowed the legend to remain relevant and captivating for modern audiences, cementing its status as a timeless folklore that continues to thrive in the digital age.

The evolution of the Jersey Devil legend exemplifies how folklore is a dynamic and ever-changing entity, molded by the cultural, social, and historical contexts in which it resides. The incorporation of local folklore, historical events, and external influences has allowed the tale to resonate with successive generations, leaving a lasting impression on the landscape of American folklore. The Jersey Devil's ability to adapt and persist over time is a testament to the enduring power of storytelling and its role in shaping our collective imagination.

The infamous "Jersey Devil sightings" of 1909 had a profound and lasting impact on the creature's legacy, solidifying its place in American folklore and popular culture. This series of reported encounters, which occurred over a period of several weeks in January 1909, captured the public's imagination and catapulted the Jersey Devil from a regional legend to a national sensation. The events of 1909 further entrenched the creature's mystique, ensuring that the legend would continue to thrive and evolve over the decades that followed.

The 1909 sightings received extensive coverage in newspapers across the United States, creating a media frenzy that captivated the nation. Sensational headlines and dramatic accounts of the creature's alleged appearances contributed to the growing interest in the legend. With each new sighting, the legend's prominence and intrigue spread far beyond the borders of New Jersey, turning the Jersey Devil into a household name.

The eyewitness testimonies and sensationalized reports from the 1909 sightings reinforced the Jersey Devil's existence in the minds of the public. While skepticism persisted, the sheer volume of reports and the credibility attributed to some eyewitnesses fueled belief in the creature's existence. As a result, the legend of the Jersey Devil gained a stronger foothold in popular consciousness and became firmly ingrained in American folklore.

Following the 1909 sightings, interest in the Jersey Devil and the Pine Barrens as a whole surged. People from all over the country flocked to the region in search of the elusive creature, hoping to catch a glimpse of the legendary being. Local businesses capitalized on this newfound tourism, offering guided tours and souvenir trinkets related to the Devil. The creature's image was plastered on postcards, advertisements, and promotional materials, further perpetuating its reputation and contributing to the economy of the area.

The 1909 sightings propelled the Jersey Devil into popular culture, inspiring numerous books, articles, and creative works centered around the creature. It became a recurring theme in literature, music, art, and movies, ensuring its presence in mainstream entertainment for decades to come. The legend of the Jersey Devil became a source of inspiration for horror enthusiasts and fantasy aficionados alike, adding to its enduring legacy as a cultural icon.

HAUNTED BY THE JERSEY DEVIL: A JOURNEY INTO AMERICAN FOLKLORE

Even after the 1909 incidents, reports of Jersey Devil sightings continued to surface periodically. The legacy of the 1909 events contributed to the enduring belief in the creature's existence among some communities. Sightings and encounters, whether genuine or not, kept the legend alive and fueled ongoing interest in the Devil, contributing to its continued presence in American folklore.

The infamous 1909 "Jersey Devil sightings" had a far-reaching impact on the creature's legacy. The intense media coverage, reinforcement of the legend, boost in tourism, and influence on popular culture all combined to cement the Jersey Devil's status as one of the most enduring and captivating figures in American folklore. The events of 1909 ensured that the tale of the Jersey Devil would persist through generations, leaving an indelible mark on the landscape of American folklore and perpetuating the fascination with the enigmatic creature.

Chapter 2: Folktales and Local Beliefs

The Jersey Devil, being a prominent figure in American folklore, has inspired a myriad of folktales and regional beliefs throughout its long history. These diverse stories often vary based on the specific community, local customs, and individual perspectives. Documenting all of them would be an extensive task, but there are some notable examples that have emerged over time.

Communities within and around the Pine Barrens of New Jersey have shared numerous accounts of sightings and encounters with the Jersey Devil. These stories often describe eerie encounters in the dark woods or unexplained occurrences attributed to the creature. Witnesses recount sightings of a winged, devilish figure flying overhead or lurking in the shadows, leaving a lasting impression on their memories and beliefs.

One of the most popular origin stories of the Jersey Devil revolves around the Leeds family curse. This tale centers on Mother Leeds, a woman who allegedly gave birth to the Devil, cursed by her own frustration and anger. The story portrays the Devil as a tragic figure, forever destined to roam the Pine Barrens as a result of its human mother's ill-fated words.

In some versions of the legend, the Jersey Devil is depicted as a guardian or protector of the Pine Barrens. It is said to protect the fragile ecosystem and the wildlife residing within, and some locals view its presence as a symbol of the region's natural beauty and resilience.

For others, the appearance of the Jersey Devil is seen as an omen of impending disaster or misfortune. Sightings of the creature are said to precede major events such as storms, accidents, or other calamities, contributing to a sense of fear and foreboding.

In certain folktales, the Jersey Devil is portrayed as a trickster figure, known to play pranks on unsuspecting humans. These stories often emphasize its cunning and mischievous nature, adding complexity to the creature's characterization.

An alternate version of the origin story suggests that the Jersey Devil was not cursed or born from malevolence but was instead an abandoned child, raised by animals in the wild. This portrayal presents the creature as more sympathetic and misunderstood, evoking themes of isolation and belonging.

In some tales, the Jersey Devil is depicted in conjunction with other supernatural beings or entities. These encounters range from eerie alliances with witches to confrontations with other mythical creatures, creating a rich and interconnected folkloric universe.

There are stories that recount individuals who, after encountering the Jersey Devil, undergo strange transformations or experiences. These accounts often explore themes of identity, self-discovery, and the blurred lines between reality and the supernatural.

HAUNTED BY THE JERSEY DEVIL: A JOURNEY INTO AMERICAN FOLKLORE

Many of these folktales have been passed down through generations within families and communities, shared during gatherings, storytelling sessions, and around campfires. This oral tradition has played a crucial role in preserving and perpetuating the legend of the Jersey Devil.

The diverse folktales and regional beliefs related to the Jersey Devil reveal the breadth of human imagination and the cultural significance of this iconic creature. Each tale reflects the unique perspectives and values of the communities from which they originate, contributing to the enduring allure of the Jersey Devil in American folklore. These stories not only entertain and intrigue but also provide valuable insights into the complexities of human beliefs and the enduring power of mythical beings in shaping our understanding of the world.

Interview locals and descendants of those who claim to have encountered the creature, collecting first-hand accounts.

The Jersey Devil legend has been retold and adapted in various ways across different New Jersey communities, leading to the emergence of diverse versions of the tale. While the core elements of the story remain consistent, regional nuances and local beliefs have influenced how the legend is interpreted and presented.

In the Pine Barrens, where the legend originated, the tale of the Jersey Devil often carries a strong sense of cultural identity. Here, the creature is frequently depicted as a protector of the wilderness, safeguarding the delicate ecosystem and maintaining balance in nature. Locals may regard the Devil with a mix of fear and respect, viewing it as a mysterious and elusive guardian of their homeland.

In coastal towns near the Pine Barrens, the Jersey Devil legend may be intertwined with tales of sea monsters and maritime folklore. The creature's appearances are sometimes linked to storms or shipwrecks, adding an additional layer of mystery and danger to the legend. The Devil is often portrayed as a malevolent force capable of bringing misfortune to sailors and fishermen.

In suburban areas of New Jersey, the Jersey Devil legend may take on a more mythical and fantastical tone. The creature is sometimes depicted as a mythical being, emerging from an ancient curse or forgotten realm. In these versions, the Devil's appearances are shrouded in magic and mysticism, appealing to audiences who enjoy fantasy storytelling.

In urban settings, the Jersey Devil legend can be interpreted in a modern context, blending elements of folklore with urban legends and paranormal experiences. Sightings and encounters with the creature are often associated with abandoned buildings, dark alleys, or eerie urban landscapes. These versions of the tale tap into the fear of the unknown and the supernatural in the city environment.

Some Native American communities in New Jersey may have their own interpretations of the Jersey Devil legend, incorporating elements of their traditional beliefs and cosmology. In these versions, the creature's origins and motivations may be tied to Native American spirits or mythological beings, providing a unique perspective on the legend.

In areas heavily reliant on tourism, the Jersey Devil legend is often presented as a thrilling and entertaining attraction. Tours, museums, and events are designed to engage visitors with the folklore, often including theatrical reenactments or costumed performers. These versions may place more emphasis on the sensational aspects of the legend, catering to the fascination with the mysterious and otherworldly.

Despite the differences in how the legend is portrayed across different New Jersey communities, some common threads run through all versions. The central figure of the Jersey Devil remains consistent, as does its association with the Pine Barrens region. The themes of fear, mystery, and the supernatural are also prevalent throughout, highlighting the enduring appeal of the tale in captivating audiences from all walks of life. Ultimately, the diverse versions of the legend speak to the cultural richness and adaptability of folklore, reflecting the unique perspectives and values of each community that keeps the legend alive.

OLIVER LANCASTER

Chapter 3: Historical Context and Cultural Impact

The historical events surrounding the time of the Jersey Devil's emergence in the 18th century provide valuable context for understanding how the legend took root and evolved over time. The tale of the Devil emerged during a period marked by religious fervor, superstitions, and societal upheaval, which all contributed to the legend's enduring legacy in American folklore.

The early 18th century in America was a time of intense religious beliefs and practices, particularly in the predominantly Puritanical society of New Jersey. People held strong convictions about the existence of supernatural beings, including demons and witches. The idea of curses and malevolent entities was prevalent in the collective imagination, creating a fertile ground for the emergence of tales like that of the Jersey Devil.

The region of New Jersey, including the Pine Barrens, was a melting pot of diverse cultural backgrounds, with settlers from different European countries and Native American tribes coexisting. As these diverse cultural traditions blended, folkloric tales and supernatural beliefs from various sources mingled and influenced one another. The legend of the Jersey Devil likely emerged as an amalgamation of these folkloric traditions, incorporating elements from European legends, Native American myths, and local oral traditions.

The Pine Barrens, where the tale of the Jersey Devil originated, was an isolated and untamed wilderness, characterized by dense forests, marshlands, and inhospitable terrain. Early settlers often viewed such wilderness areas with fear and suspicion, associating them with danger, darkness, and the unknown. The notion of a fearsome, otherworldly creature inhabiting this desolate landscape likely tapped into these anxieties, amplifying the legend's impact.

The Leeds family, linked to the Jersey Devil legend through Mother Leeds, were actual historical figures who resided in the Pine Barrens. The folklore around the Leeds family was likely influenced by local rumors and hearsay about their eccentricities and unconventional lifestyle. Moreover, the Leeds family was also associated with political and social controversies of the time, contributing to the legend's allure and notoriety.

During the colonial era, storytelling was a significant means of entertainment and information sharing, especially in isolated communities like the Pine Barrens. Folktales and legends were often passed down orally from one generation to another, evolving and adapting as they were retold by different individuals. The Jersey Devil legend gained momentum through this oral tradition, becoming deeply ingrained in the cultural fabric of the region.

HAUNTED BY THE JERSEY DEVIL: A JOURNEY INTO AMERICAN FOLKLORE

As printing and publishing became more accessible during the 18th century, written accounts of local legends and events began to circulate in newspapers and pamphlets. These early forms of media contributed to the spread of the Jersey Devil legend beyond the confines of the Pine Barrens, reaching a wider audience and further solidifying its status as a well-known tale.

The historical events surrounding the emergence of the Jersey Devil legend in the early 18th century reveal a fascinating intersection of religious beliefs, cultural blending, fear of the unknown, and the power of oral tradition. These factors combined to create an enduring legend that has transcended time and continues to captivate audiences with its mysterious origins and eerie allure. The tale of the Jersey Devil remains a testament to the lasting impact of folklore in shaping our understanding of the past and our collective cultural identity.

The Jersey Devil's cultural impact has been profound and far-reaching, extending beyond its origins in American folklore to influence various aspects of literature, art, and popular media. As a captivating and enigmatic figure, the Devil has become an enduring symbol of the unknown, the supernatural, and the unexplained, resonating with audiences across generations and captivating the human imagination.

The Jersey Devil has been a recurring theme in literature, with numerous books, short stories, and poems featuring the creature as a central character or plot element. Authors have explored various aspects of the legend, from its origins and sightings to its interactions with humans and other mythical beings. Some works cast the Devil as a menacing antagonist, while others portray it as a misunderstood and tragic figure. Regardless of the approach, the Devil's presence in literature has added depth to the legend and allowed it to endure in the literary canon.

The visual representation of the Jersey Devil has been a subject of artistic exploration for centuries. Paintings, illustrations, and sculptures of the creature often depict it as a fearsome, winged being with demonic features, capturing the eerie essence of the legend. Artists have interpreted the Devil in various styles, from realistic and grotesque to fantastical and symbolic. These artistic representations have contributed to the creature's iconic status, leaving lasting impressions on those who encounter them.

The Jersey Devil has made significant appearances in various forms of popular media, including films, television shows, and video games. The creature has become a recurring character in horror and fantasy genres, starring in movies that either reinterpret the legend or offer creative adaptations. Television shows have featured episodes centered around the Devil, further cementing its place in modern pop culture. In video games, the creature serves as a formidable adversary or an enigmatic presence in the game's narrative, adding an element of mystery and suspense.

The legend of the Jersey Devil has become an integral part of New Jersey's cultural identity and a source of tourism revenue. Guided tours, museums, and events dedicated to the Devil draw visitors from all over, seeking to experience the allure of the legend firsthand. Souvenirs, postcards, and memorabilia featuring the creature are widely available, serving as tangible reminders of the Devil's impact on the region's culture and economy.

The rise of the internet and social media has further extended the Jersey Devil's cultural impact. Online communities discuss the legend, share alleged sightings, and speculate on its origins and significance. The Devil's presence in internet forums, social media groups, and YouTube videos keeps the legend alive in the digital age and allows it to reach new audiences worldwide.

The Jersey Devil's cultural impact has transcended its origins in folklore to become a multi-faceted and enduring figure in literature, art, and popular media. Its appearances in various creative works and its influence on tourism and merchandising attest to the enduring fascination with this enigmatic creature. Whether portrayed as a fearsome monster, a misunderstood entity, or a symbol of the unknown, the Jersey Devil's presence in cultural expressions continues to reflect the human fascination with the supernatural and the enduring power of mythical creatures in shaping our collective imagination.

In modern-day pop culture, the Jersey Devil remains a captivating and influential figure that continues to capture the public imagination. Its enduring presence in various forms of media, entertainment, and popular discourse speaks to the creature's iconic status as a symbol of the unknown and the supernatural.

The Jersey Devil has been featured in numerous films and television shows, often serving as a central plot element in horror, fantasy, and supernatural genres. These appearances range from low-budget horror films to high-profile productions, showcasing the creature's versatility as a source of suspense and terror. The Devil's enigmatic nature and mysterious origins make it a compelling antagonist or a captivating enigma for filmmakers and TV producers to explore.

The legend of the Jersey Devil continues to inspire authors and writers to craft compelling stories and novels. The creature's presence in literature extends beyond traditional folktales and now includes works that reinterpret or reimagine the legend in modern settings. Such literary adaptations allow for fresh perspectives and creative exploration of the Devil's character and its place in contemporary society.

The internet has provided a platform for enthusiasts and believers of the Jersey Devil to share their stories, sightings, and theories. Online communities, forums, and social media groups dedicated to the creature allow people from all over the world to engage in discussions, further fueling its enduring appeal. Memes, fan art, and fictional accounts featuring the Devil are also prevalent online, adding to its presence in digital culture.

The Jersey Devil's impact on New Jersey's tourism industry remains significant. Guided tours, museums, and festivals dedicated to the legend attract visitors eager to experience the folklore in person. The creature's image appears on a wide array of merchandise, from t-shirts and mugs to keychains and magnets, making it a recognizable and marketable symbol of the region's cultural heritage.

The Jersey Devil is a subject of interest in the field of cryptozoology and paranormal investigations. Cryptozoologists study creatures from folklore and legends, seeking evidence of their existence. The legend of the Jersey Devil has also caught the attention of paranormal investigators who explore sightings and encounters related to the creature, adding a layer of intrigue and mystery to its status as an enigmatic being.

Educational platforms, such as podcasts and documentary series, have dedicated episodes to exploring the Jersey Devil legend. These formats offer a mix of historical research, eyewitness accounts, and expert insights, helping to disseminate knowledge about the folklore while keeping the creature alive in the public consciousness.

The Jersey Devil's place in modern-day pop culture reflects its enduring power to captivate the public imagination. Whether it appears in horror films, online discussions, paranormal investigations, or tourist attractions, the creature's enigmatic nature and the rich tapestry of its legend continue to enthrall audiences. The Devil's adaptability to various media and its ability to resonate with contemporary audiences reaffirm its status as an iconic figure in American folklore, demonstrating that mythical creatures like the Jersey Devil have an enduring place in shaping our cultural identity and fascination with the unknown.

Chapter 4: Cryptozoology and Scientific Perspectives

C ryptozoology is a field of study that focuses on investigating and researching animals that are considered to be legendary, mythical, or cryptids. These creatures, known as cryptids, are beings whose existence is based on folklore, eyewitness accounts, or unverified evidence rather than established scientific knowledge. Cryptozoologists seek to gather evidence and evaluate the plausibility of these cryptids' existence, often challenging conventional scientific paradigms.

The connection between cryptozoology and the study of mythical creatures like the Jersey Devil lies in their shared status as enigmatic and elusive beings. While mythical creatures are often rooted in folklore and cultural traditions, they exist as legendary beings rather than proven entities. Cryptozoology, on the other hand, is a scientific pursuit that seeks to explore the possibility of cryptids' existence through empirical investigation and evidence collection.

The Jersey Devil is a prime example of a cryptid that has piqued the interest of cryptozoologists. Sightings and encounters with the creature have been reported for centuries, fueling curiosity and speculation about its existence. Cryptozoologists investigate these accounts, collecting data, analyzing witness testimonies, and exploring the ecological plausibility of the Devil's alleged habitat and behavior. They seek to understand whether the creature could potentially be a surviving, undiscovered species or an entirely new form of life.

It's important to note that cryptozoology is not universally accepted as a mainstream scientific discipline. Critics argue that the field often relies on anecdotal evidence, lacks rigorous scientific methodologies, and can perpetuate pseudoscientific claims. The study of cryptids can also be prone to sensationalism, leading to the uncritical acceptance of extraordinary claims without proper scrutiny.

Despite these criticisms, cryptozoologists play an essential role in cultural and anthropological research. Their investigations into folklore and the cultural significance of mythical creatures shed light on the ways in which humans perceive and interact with the natural world. Additionally, cryptozoological inquiries can occasionally lead to the discovery of previously unknown species, as has happened with various animals previously considered cryptids, like the okapi and the coelacanth.

Cryptozoology is a field that bridges the gap between scientific inquiry and cultural exploration, aiming to investigate and understand legendary creatures like the Jersey Devil. While some consider it a fringe or speculative field, cryptozoologists continue to explore the unknown, fostering a fascination with cryptids and their potential place in our understanding of the natural world. The quest to unveil the truth behind mythical beings reflects humanity's enduring curiosity about the mysteries that lie beyond the boundaries of established science.

HAUNTED BY THE JERSEY DEVIL: A JOURNEY INTO AMERICAN FOLKLORE

Scientific investigations into the existence of the Jersey Devil through zoological and ecological lenses have largely sought to evaluate the plausibility of the creature's existence based on biological, ecological, and environmental factors. While these investigations have provided some insights, it is essential to note that the Jersey Devil remains a cryptid, and no concrete scientific evidence confirming its existence has been found to date.

From a zoological perspective, researchers have attempted to determine whether the Jersey Devil could be a biological entity, such as an unknown species of animal. Some have proposed that the creature might be an undiscovered species of bat, bird, or large bird-like animal. They argue that unusual physical characteristics attributed to the Jersey Devil, such as wings and hooves, might be misinterpretations or exaggerations of more common features found in known animals.

Ecological studies have focused on evaluating the feasibility of sustaining a population of creatures like the Jersey Devil in the Pine Barrens and its surrounding areas. Researchers have examined the available resources, habitat suitability, and ecological niches that could potentially support an undiscovered species. However, the dense and isolated nature of the Pine Barrens has also made it difficult to conduct comprehensive surveys and studies.

Skeptics and researchers have pointed to the possibility of misidentifications or mistaken interpretations of natural phenomena as potential explanations for Jersey Devil sightings. They suggest that sightings of the creature may be sightings of known animals behaving unusually, such as owls, large birds, or other wildlife. Additionally, folklore and cultural beliefs surrounding the creature may have contributed to the perpetuation of the legend, leading to an exaggeration of reported encounters.

Researchers in psychology and sociology have explored how collective beliefs and cultural factors influence the perception and belief in mythical creatures like the Jersey Devil. They have studied how local folklore, storytelling, and community beliefs contribute to the legend's longevity and continued impact on the public imagination.

Scientists have recognized the significance of the Jersey Devil in local culture and its role as a cultural symbol for the people of New Jersey. Understanding the cultural importance of the legend helps contextualize its persistence and continued fascination among local communities.

Scientific investigations into the existence of the Jersey Devil have primarily attempted to evaluate the legend through zoological and ecological perspectives. While these efforts have shed light on possible explanations for reported sightings and encounters, the scientific consensus remains that there is no concrete evidence supporting the existence of the Jersey Devil as a biological entity. As with many cryptids, the legend of the Jersey Devil continues to thrive as a cultural phenomenon, attracting interest from both believers and skeptics alike, and leaving the creature's true nature shrouded in mystery.

Potential explanations for sightings and encounters of the Jersey Devil, including misidentifications and natural phenomena, have been subjects of investigation and skepticism among researchers and skeptics. While these explanations may not account for all reported encounters, they provide alternative perspectives on the origin of the legend.

Some of the potential explanations include:

1. Misidentifications of Wildlife:

Many sightings of the Jersey Devil could be attributed to misidentifications of known wildlife, especially in low-light or fleeting encounters. Large birds, such as owls or herons, can appear formidable and even eerie when seen at a distance or in dim light. Additionally, other animals like deer, dogs, or even feral pigs may be mistaken for the creature, especially if viewed from a distance or under stressful conditions.

2. Barn Owls:

Barn owls, with their distinctive heart-shaped facial disc and eerie calls, are often suggested as a potential source for Jersey Devil sightings. Barn owls are nocturnal creatures that are known to inhabit wooded areas, and their flight pattern and appearance in flight might resemble descriptions of the Devil in some accounts.

3. Flocks of Birds:

Large flocks of birds flying together can create striking and unexpected sights, especially in low light. A flock of birds silhouetted against the night sky might appear as a single large creature with outstretched wings, leading to reports of a winged creature like the Jersey Devil.

4. Atmospheric and Weather Phenomena:

Unusual atmospheric conditions or weather phenomena, such as strange cloud formations, optical illusions, or mirages, could contribute to sightings of strange shapes and figures in the sky. Under specific weather conditions, certain optical illusions might make natural objects appear distorted or bizarre, potentially contributing to perceptions of the Devil's unusual appearance.

5. Pranks and Hoaxes:

Throughout history, there have been cases of pranks and hoaxes involving the Jersey Devil, where individuals fabricate sightings or encounters for attention or amusement. These fabricated stories can spread through oral tradition or media, contributing to the legend's perpetuation.

6. Cultural and Psychological Factors:

Cultural beliefs, superstitions, and collective imagination can influence how individuals perceive and interpret their experiences. In communities with a rich tradition of the Jersey Devil legend, such beliefs might shape how people interpret unusual or unexplained events, leading to attributions of the creature's presence.

7. Pareidolia:

HAUNTED BY THE JERSEY DEVIL: A JOURNEY INTO AMERICAN FOLKLORE

Pareidolia is a psychological phenomenon where the human brain perceives familiar patterns or shapes in random stimuli, such as clouds, shadows, or natural formations. This psychological tendency could lead individuals to perceive the outline of a winged creature in otherwise ordinary shapes or phenomena.

Potential explanations for sightings and encounters of the Jersey Devil often involve misidentifications of known animals, natural phenomena, or psychological factors. While these explanations offer plausible alternatives to the creature's existence, they do not diminish the cultural significance of the legend or the enduring fascination it holds for believers and skeptics alike. The Jersey Devil continues to capture the public imagination, and the mystery surrounding its origin remains an enduring aspect of American folklore.

Chapter 5: Historical Sightings and Unexplained Incidents

The sightings listed here are based on historical accounts and folklore, but their authenticity remains a subject of debate. This list includes some of the most notable documented Jersey Devil sightings throughout history:

1. 1735: The Leeds Family Legend

One of the earliest accounts of the Jersey Devil dates back to 1735, with the legend of Mother Leeds. According to the tale, Mother Leeds, a resident of the Pine Barrens, cursed her 13th child during childbirth, leading to the creature's birth. This legend forms the foundation of the Jersey Devil's origin story.

2. Early 1800s: The Commodore Stephen Decatur Sighting

In the early 1800s, it was reported that Commodore Stephen Decatur, a naval hero, encountered a strange winged creature while visiting the Hanover Mill Works in New Jersey. Decatur allegedly fired at the creature but did not succeed in capturing it.

3. Late 1800s: Joseph Bonaparte's Sighting

Joseph Bonaparte, the elder brother of Napoleon Bonaparte and former King of Naples and Spain, is said to have seen the Jersey Devil during his time living in New Jersey.

4. 1909: The "Jersey Devil Sighting" Flap

One of the most well-documented periods of sightings occurred in January 1909 when numerous reports emerged from various locations in New Jersey and neighboring states. Hundreds of people claimed to have seen a winged creature resembling the Jersey Devil. Newspapers covered the phenomenon extensively, fueling public interest in the legend.

5. 1927: The "Emil Schatz" Photograph

In 1927, a photograph taken by amateur photographer Emil Schatz gained attention. The image purportedly showed the Jersey Devil perched on a fence, although many experts and skeptics questioned its authenticity.

6. 1951: The McOwen Family Sighting

The McOwen family of Gibbstown, New Jersey, claimed to have seen the Jersey Devil in 1951. They described the creature as having "glowing red eyes" and making a "weird sound" before flying away.

7. 1960s: Sightings by New Jersey Residents

Throughout the 1960s, there were numerous reports of Jersey Devil sightings by residents in different parts of New Jersey, including the Pine Barrens and surrounding areas.

8. 2015: The Blackwood Jersey Devil Sighting

In 2015, a video emerged showing a strange figure resembling the Jersey Devil flying across the sky in Blackwood, New Jersey.

HAUNTED BY THE JERSEY DEVIL: A JOURNEY INTO AMERICAN FOLKLORE

The video sparked new interest in the legend but was met with skepticism by many.

Please keep in mind that the above list only represents a selection of documented sightings reported over the years. Many more alleged sightings exist in local folklore and oral traditions, contributing to the enduring fascination with the Jersey Devil legend. As a legendary creature, the Jersey Devil's existence remains unproven, and the sightings listed here are subject to interpretation and debate.

Over the years, numerous experts, researchers, and investigators have explored the alleged encounters and unexplained incidents surrounding the legend of the Jersey Devil. These individuals have approached the topic from various perspectives, including folklore studies, cryptozoology, paranormal investigations, and cultural anthropology. While opinions on the Jersey Devil's existence vary, these experts have contributed to the ongoing dialogue surrounding the legend. Here are some notable researchers who have studied the Jersey Devil:

1. Loren Coleman:

Loren Coleman is a well-known cryptozoologist and author who has extensively researched and written about various cryptids, including the Jersey Devil. He has contributed to the field of cryptozoology, investigating reports of mythical creatures and investigating claims related to the Jersey Devil.

2. Brian Regal:

Brian Regal is a historian and folklorist known for his expertise in studying legends and mythical creatures. He has written extensively on the subject of the Jersey Devil and has researched the historical origins and cultural significance of the legend.

3. Mark Moran and Mark Sceurman:

Moran and Sceurman are the authors of "Weird NJ," a publication that delves into unusual and paranormal stories in New Jersey, including the Jersey Devil legend. Their work has brought attention to local folklore and unexplained incidents in the state.

4. Chad Lewis:

Chad Lewis is a paranormal investigator and researcher who has explored various supernatural phenomena, including the Jersey Devil sightings. His investigations often involve interviewing eyewitnesses and examining historical records to provide insights into the folklore and legends surrounding the creature.

5. Joseph Laycock:

Joseph Laycock is a religious studies scholar who has written about various topics related to the supernatural, including folklore and cryptozoology. He has discussed the Jersey Devil as part of his research on American religious and cultural beliefs.

6. University Scholars and Historians:

HAUNTED BY THE JERSEY DEVIL: A JOURNEY INTO AMERICAN FOLKLORE

Academics from various universities have also contributed to the study of the Jersey Devil legend. Folklorists, historians, and cultural anthropologists have examined the cultural significance of the creature and its impact on local communities in New Jersey.

7. Paranormal Investigators and Local Enthusiasts:

Various paranormal investigation teams and local enthusiasts have conducted their own research on the Jersey Devil. They often venture into the Pine Barrens and surrounding areas to interview witnesses, explore historical sites, and document alleged encounters with the creature.

It's important to note that opinions on the Jersey Devil's existence and significance differ among these researchers. Some approach the topic with skepticism, viewing the creature as a product of folklore and cultural beliefs, while others maintain an open-minded perspective, investigating alleged sightings and exploring possible scientific explanations. The work of these experts and researchers has contributed to a deeper understanding of the legend's cultural impact and the enduring fascination with mythical creatures like the Jersey Devil.

Analyzing patterns and commonalities among reported sightings of the Jersey Devil can offer insights into the creature's alleged behavior, characteristics, and the cultural factors influencing the legend. While the following analysis is based on historical accounts and folklore, it can provide a better understanding of the recurring themes associated with the creature.

The majority of reported sightings are concentrated in and around the Pine Barrens of New Jersey, particularly in areas with dense forests and marshlands. This suggests that the alleged behavior of the Jersey Devil is closely tied to its habitat, with sightings occurring in the wilderness and remote regions.

Many accounts describe the Jersey Devil as a nocturnal creature, appearing predominantly at night. This aligns with typical behaviors of known nocturnal animals, which are more active during the nighttime hours.

A common feature in sightings is the creature's description as a winged being, often resembling a large bird or bat. Witnesses report the creature flying or gliding through the air, consistent with the portrayal of the Jersey Devil as an aerial creature.

Numerous sightings involve descriptions of eerie sounds and calls attributed to the Jersey Devil. Witnesses often report hearing shrieks, howls, or screeches that are distinctive and unsettling. These auditory aspects contribute to the creature's fearsome reputation.

A consistent detail in sightings is the mention of the creature's eyes, often described as glowing red or possessing an unnatural luminescence. This feature adds to the creature's eerie and otherworldly appearance.

Witnesses commonly describe the Jersey Devil as large and intimidating, with some accounts claiming it to be as tall as a man or larger. The creature's imposing size contributes to the fear and awe it elicits.

Several accounts suggest that the Jersey Devil moves with agility and speed, making it difficult to track or capture. Witnesses often describe the creature vanishing into the wilderness after brief encounters, leaving a sense of mystery and elusiveness.

Some sightings of the Jersey Devil are associated with specific natural events, such as storms, lunar cycles, or seasonal changes. These connections may be linked to cultural beliefs and superstitions, adding an element of mysticism to the creature's alleged behavior.

There are reports of seasonal variations in Jersey Devil sightings, with some accounts suggesting higher frequencies of encounters during specific times of the year. These patterns might be influenced by migratory behaviors of animals or cultural traditions tied to specific seasons.

Overall, the commonalities among reported sightings paint a picture of the Jersey Devil as a mysterious, nocturnal, and aerial creature with an eerie presence. The creature's alleged behavior aligns with the characteristics of legendary beings found in folklore and traditional tales. While these patterns offer intriguing insights, it is essential to remember that the Jersey Devil remains a legendary figure, and the accounts are subject to interpretation, cultural influences, and the power of storytelling in shaping the legend's narrative.

Chapter 6: Legends from the Pines

The Pine Barrens of New Jersey serves as the primary location for the majority of reported Jersey Devil sightings, making it the epicenter of the legend's alleged activity. This vast and remote region, covering over one million acres, is characterized by dense pine forests, wetlands, and sandy soil, creating an ideal habitat for various wildlife and contributing to the aura of mystery and wilderness that surrounds the Jersey Devil legend. Several factors associated with the Pine Barrens contribute to the prevalence of sightings and the enduring fascination with the creature.

The Pine Barrens is sparsely populated and has vast uninhabited areas, providing a sense of isolation and desolation. This remoteness enhances the allure of the region and contributes to the idea that the area is a fitting dwelling place for mythical creatures like the Jersey Devil.

The dense pine forests and marshy wetlands create a dark and eerie atmosphere, particularly at night. The combination of shadows and the rustling of trees can evoke feelings of apprehension and lend credence to sightings of mysterious and otherworldly creatures.

The Pine Barrens has a rich history of folklore and cultural beliefs, which have contributed to the perpetuation of the Jersey Devil legend. Tales of the Devil have been passed down through generations, entwining the creature with the region's cultural identity.

The legend of the Jersey Devil is deeply rooted in the history of the Pine Barrens. The story of Mother Leeds and her cursed 13th child, said to have given birth to the creature, is intrinsically tied to the region's lore.

The Pine Barrens is home to a diverse array of wildlife, including various bird species, bats, and other creatures. Misidentifications of these animals may have contributed to some reported sightings of the Jersey Devil.

The prevalence of Jersey Devil sightings has transformed the Pine Barrens into a popular tourist attraction for enthusiasts, paranormal investigators, and those curious about the legend. Guided tours and events centered around the creature further perpetuate its presence in the region.

The Pine Barrens' reputation as a mysterious and enigmatic wilderness appeals to adventurous individuals seeking to explore the unknown. The prospect of encountering a legendary creature like the Jersey Devil adds to the region's allure.

The Pine Barrens of New Jersey holds a central place in the Jersey Devil legend due to its eerie and isolated landscape, historical significance, cultural beliefs, and diverse wildlife. The region's mystique has contributed to numerous reported sightings and encounters with the legendary creature, making it a focal point for those interested in exploring the mysteries of the Jersey Devil and the enduring allure of folklore and the unknown.

The Pine Barrens of New Jersey holds significant importance in local folklore, history, and culture, and it is closely associated with various supernatural entities, including the legendary Jersey Devil. The region's unique landscape, isolation, and mysterious ambiance have contributed to the development of a rich tapestry of myths and legends that have been passed down through generations.

The Pine Barrens has long been associated with mythical creatures and legends, with the Jersey Devil being the most prominent example. The legend of the Jersey Devil is deeply rooted in the folklore of the region and has become an integral part of its cultural identity. The Devil's supposed haunts and sightings in the Pine Barrens have been recounted in numerous stories, oral traditions, and books, shaping the region's collective imagination.

The vastness and isolation of the Pine Barrens have contributed to its reputation as a wild and mysterious place. The dense forests, vast swamps, and winding trails create an aura of solitude and otherness, making it an ideal setting for stories of supernatural beings and unexplained phenomena.

The Pine Barrens' historical isolation has allowed for the preservation of unique cultural beliefs and superstitions. The folklore of the region has often served as a way for communities to explain the unexplainable, such as unusual natural occurrences or unexplained sounds. Beliefs in supernatural entities like the Jersey Devil have become embedded in local customs and traditions, becoming an essential part of the cultural fabric of the area.

In addition to the Jersey Devil, the Pine Barrens is associated with other paranormal and ghostly tales. Stories of haunted houses, eerie apparitions, and ghostly lights add to the region's allure and contribute to its reputation as a hotbed of supernatural activity.

The Pine Barrens' mysterious and haunting qualities have inspired numerous writers, artists, and filmmakers over the years. The region's rich folklore, including the legend of the Jersey Devil, has served as a backdrop for various works of fiction, horror stories, and visual art.

The significance of the Pine Barrens in local folklore has contributed to the region's appeal as a tourist destination. Visitors are drawn to explore the mysteries and legends associated with the area, taking part in guided tours and events centered around the Jersey Devil and other supernatural entities.

The Pine Barrens of New Jersey holds a special place in local folklore and culture, with its association with supernatural entities like the Jersey Devil contributing to its mystique and allure. The region's unique landscape, isolation, and rich history have fostered a wealth of myths and legends that continue to captivate the imagination of locals and visitors alike. The folklore surrounding the Pine Barrens serves as a reminder of the enduring power of storytelling and its role in shaping the cultural identity of a region.

The environment, particularly the Pine Barrens of New Jersey, has played a crucial role in perpetuating the Jersey Devil legend. The unique landscape, isolation, and eerie ambiance of the region have contributed to the creation, dissemination, and endurance of the folklore surrounding the creature. Several factors related to the environment have influenced the legend's perpetuation.

The Pine Barrens' vast expanse of dense forests, marshlands, and sandy soil creates an atmosphere of mystery and isolation. The region's remote and largely uninhabited areas have been fertile ground for tales of mythical creatures and unexplained phenomena, contributing to the legend's origin and ongoing fascination.

The unfamiliarity of the Pine Barrens' landscape for many outsiders has added to the allure of the region as a place of wonder and fear. The terrain's foreboding nature has inspired stories of hidden dangers and uncharted territories, fostering an environment conducive to the development of legendary creatures like the Jersey Devil.

The Pine Barrens has a rich history of folklore and cultural identity tied to the Jersey Devil legend. Tales of the creature have been passed down through generations, creating a strong cultural attachment to the myth within local communities. The storytelling tradition keeps the legend alive and contributes to its perpetuation.

The changing seasons and natural phenomena in the Pine Barrens have been incorporated into the Jersey Devil legend. Seasonal variations in sightings and associations with specific natural events add depth to the folklore and contribute to the belief in the creature's existence.

The Pine Barrens, with its diverse wildlife and natural beauty, provides a fitting habitat for the Jersey Devil's alleged behavior. Reports of eerie sounds, winged creatures, and mysterious sightings align with the region's environmental characteristics, reinforcing the legend's credibility in the eyes of believers.

The perpetuation of the Jersey Devil legend has become a cultural tourism attraction, drawing visitors intrigued by the folklore to the Pine Barrens. Guided tours, museums, and events centered around the creature contribute to the local economy and reinforce the legend's significance in the region's cultural heritage.

The portrayal of the Pine Barrens and the Jersey Devil in various forms of media and popular culture has further perpetuated the legend. Books, films, television shows, and online content have extended the creature's reach beyond local folklore, introducing it to a global audience.

The environment of the Pine Barrens, with its mysterious and isolated wilderness, historical folklore, cultural identity, and associations with natural phenomena, has been a foundational factor in perpetuating the Jersey Devil legend. The region's aura of mystery and foreboding has fueled belief in the creature's existence, while its cultural significance has ensured that the legend remains deeply embedded in the local tradition and continues to captivate the public imagination. As long as the Pine Barrens retains its allure as a place of enigma and wonder, the Jersey Devil legend will endure as a testament to the enduring power of folklore and storytelling.

Chapter 7: Hoaxes and Pranks

Throughout the history of the Jersey Devil legend, there have been several instances of hoaxes and pranks related to the creature. These fabrications, whether for entertainment, attention, or other motives, have contributed to the folklore's complexity and the challenge of distinguishing fact from fiction. Here are some notable instances of hoaxes and pranks associated with the Jersey Devil:

1. The "Leeds Devil" Carnival Hoax (1909):

During the infamous "Jersey Devil sightings" flap of 1909, a group of pranksters capitalized on the hysteria by creating a carnival attraction featuring a fake Jersey Devil. The creature was a grotesque, fabricated figure designed to mimic eyewitness descriptions and capitalize on public interest. The Leeds Devil Carnival became a popular attraction during the period but further blurred the line between truth and fiction surrounding the legend.

2. The "Emil Schatz" Jersey Devil Photograph (1927):

In 1927, a photograph purportedly taken by Emil Schatz, an amateur photographer, surfaced, showing the Jersey Devil perched on a fence. The image gained attention and was published in newspapers, but it was later revealed to be a cleverly crafted hoax. The photograph was likely a composite or manipulated image, raising skepticism about other visual evidence related to the Jersey Devil.

3. Mischief Night Pranks:

Mischief Night, a tradition in some areas where pranks are played the night before Halloween, has led to various instances of Jersey Devil-related hoaxes. People have dressed up as the creature and staged fake sightings or encounters to spook others and add to the legend's allure.

4. Social Media and Online Hoaxes:

With the advent of social media and online platforms, hoaxes related to the Jersey Devil have become more prevalent. Photos, videos, and accounts of alleged sightings are often shared and circulated, making it difficult to discern genuine reports from fabricated ones. Some individuals create elaborate stories or use photo-editing tools to add a sense of authenticity to their claims.

5. Local Legends and Tall Tales:

Within local communities, stories and tall tales of encounters with the Jersey Devil have been used to entertain and amuse, blurring the line between genuine belief and playful storytelling. These legends often involve exaggerated or humorous accounts of supposed sightings and encounters with the creature.

6. Fictional Literature and Media:

Authors and filmmakers have also contributed to the perpetuation of the Jersey Devil legend through works of fiction and horror. While not hoaxes in the traditional sense, these creative interpretations can blur the line between fact and fiction and influence public perceptions of the creature.

It's important to note that while hoaxes and pranks have added layers of complexity to the Jersey Devil legend, they do not negate the genuine belief and folklore surrounding the creature. The enduring fascination with the Jersey Devil continues to draw interest from believers, skeptics, and curious individuals alike, demonstrating the power of folklore and urban legends in shaping cultural identities and stimulating the human imagination.

The hoaxes and pranks related to the Jersey Devil have had a significant impact on public perception of the creature and its legitimacy. These fabrications, whether intentional or unintentional, have added to the complexity and skepticism surrounding the legend.

Repeated instances of hoaxes, especially in the age of digital media, have led to increased skepticism among the general public. As hoaxes are exposed and shared widely, people become more cautious about accepting new claims of Jersey Devil sightings or encounters at face value. The prevalence of online misinformation and photo-editing tools has further fueled doubts about the legitimacy of alleged evidence.

Hoaxes have blurred the line between fact and fiction in the Jersey Devil legend. The Leeds Devil Carnival attraction and the "Emil Schatz" photograph are just two examples of how fabricated visual evidence and staged encounters have contributed to the folklore's complexity. These instances make it challenging for individuals to distinguish genuine accounts from elaborate pranks.

Even legitimate witness testimonies of Jersey Devil sightings can be met with skepticism due to the prevalence of hoaxes and fabricated encounters. As a result, individuals who genuinely believe they have seen something unusual may be hesitant to share their experiences, fearing ridicule or dismissal.

The proliferation of hoaxes has also affected how academics and scientists approach the Jersey Devil legend. The presence of numerous fabricated stories and misleading visual evidence has made it more challenging to conduct credible research and separate genuine historical records from fictional accounts.

Hoaxes related to the Jersey Devil have become a part of popular culture and entertainment. Fictional works, documentaries, and online content often reference these pranks, leading some to view the entire legend as a creative invention rather than a subject worthy of serious investigation.

While hoaxes can create skepticism, they also contribute to public interest and tourism surrounding the Jersey Devil legend. The allure of mystery and fascination with the creature's folklore still attract enthusiasts, paranormal investigators, and curious visitors to the Pine Barrens and the surrounding areas.

The influence of hoaxes and pranks on the Jersey Devil legend has both positive and negative consequences. While they have contributed to public skepticism and blurred the line between fact and fiction, they have also helped maintain the creature's status as an enduring cultural icon and tourist attraction. The challenge lies in striking a balance between appreciating the folklore's significance and critically examining the available evidence to explore the creature's origins and cultural impact.

Perpetrators of hoaxes related to the Jersey Devil have been driven by various motivations, ranging from seeking attention and amusement to capitalizing on public interest and folklore. The impact of these hoaxes on the folklore surrounding the Jersey Devil has been multifaceted, shaping public perception, contributing to the legend's complexity, and influencing the cultural significance of the creature. Let's delve into the motivations behind perpetrating such hoaxes and their impact on the folklore:

Motivations behind perpetrating hoaxes:

1. ATTENTION-SEEKING: Some individuals create Jersey Devil hoaxes to garner attention and notoriety. Fabricating sightings or encounters with the creature can attract media attention, social media shares, and public curiosity, offering a moment of fame for those involved.

2. Humor and Prankster Culture: Hoaxes can be motivated by a desire to entertain or prank others. Some individuals enjoy playing practical jokes, and the Jersey Devil legend presents a captivating and mysterious subject for creative mischief.

3. Profit and Tourism: For certain businesses and attractions in the Pine Barrens area, associating with the Jersey Devil legend can draw in tourists and generate revenue. Hoaxes or exaggerated stories can be employed as promotional tools to attract visitors and enthusiasts.

4. Social Media and Internet Culture: The ease of sharing information on social media platforms has contributed to the proliferation of hoaxes. Creating and sharing fabricated Jersey Devil sightings or encounters can be done quickly and reach a vast audience, feeding into internet culture and viral content.

Impact on the folklore surrounding the Jersey Devil:

1. SKEPTICISM AND CREDIBILITY: Hoaxes have led to increased skepticism surrounding the Jersey Devil legend. The prevalence of fabricated stories and visual evidence can make it challenging for individuals to determine the legitimacy of alleged sightings and encounters.

2. Complexity and Blurred Truth: The propagation of hoaxes blurs the line between fact and fiction in the folklore. As more hoaxes emerge, it becomes increasingly difficult to differentiate genuine historical records and testimonies from staged or fabricated accounts.

3. Entertainment and Tourism: Despite their potential negative impact, hoaxes have contributed to public interest and tourism surrounding the Jersey Devil legend. The allure of mystery and fascination with the creature's folklore still attracts

visitors and enthusiasts, sustaining the cultural significance of the legend.

4. Adaptation and Evolution: The spread of hoaxes has led to the adaptation and evolution of the folklore. New elements, exaggerated features, and creative interpretations can emerge from these fabricated stories, influencing the creature's portrayal in popular culture and artistic works.

5. Preservation and Legacy: In an ironic twist, the perpetuation of hoaxes has inadvertently contributed to preserving the Jersey Devil legend. The creature's enduring status as a cultural icon and tourist attraction owes, in part, to the attention garnered through both legitimate folklore and fabricated accounts.

Hoaxes related to the Jersey Devil have been motivated by attention-seeking, humor, profit, and the influence of internet culture. While these fabrications can lead to increased skepticism and blur the truth, they have also contributed to public interest, entertainment, and the folklore's legacy. The Jersey Devil legend continues to captivate the public imagination, thanks in part to the interplay between genuine folklore and the imaginative pranks that have shaped the creature's ongoing narrative.

OLIVER LANCASTER

Chapter 8: Legends of Abductions and Mysterious Disappearances

As part of the rich tapestry of the Jersey Devil legend, there are occasional stories and accounts that associate the creature with abductions and mysterious disappearances. These tales often weave elements of horror and mystery into the folklore, further heightening the creature's reputation as an enigmatic and fearsome being. It is essential to note that these stories are part of the folklore and urban legends surrounding the Jersey Devil and lack verifiable evidence.

However, they add to the creature's aura of menace and continue to capture the public imagination. Here are some common themes and examples of the Jersey Devil being associated with abductions and mysterious disappearances:

1. Abduction of Livestock and Pets:

Numerous accounts suggest that the Jersey Devil has a taste for livestock and pets. Local folklore includes stories of farmers waking up to find their animals missing, with claw marks and strange footprints left as evidence of the creature's visitation. These stories often serve as cautionary tales, warning people to take precautionary measures to protect their animals from the creature's alleged predation.

2. Abduction of Children:

Some versions of the Jersey Devil legend include stories of the creature abducting or attacking children who venture too close to its lair. These tales add a chilling dimension to the folklore, portraying the creature as a malevolent force that preys on the vulnerable.

3. Mysterious Disappearances in the Pine Barrens:

The Pine Barrens, where the majority of Jersey Devil sightings are reported, has its share of stories about mysterious disappearances. While not directly attributed to the creature in all cases, these tales often become intertwined with the legend, contributing to the region's reputation as a place of danger and intrigue.

4. Nightmarish Encounters:

Some stories recount nightmarish encounters with the Jersey Devil, where individuals claim to have been pursued or chased by the creature in the darkness. These encounters often result in individuals escaping narrowly or disappearing without a trace, adding to the air of mystery surrounding the folklore.

5. Variations in Regional Folklore:

The Jersey Devil legend has multiple variations across different communities in New Jersey. Each version may include unique elements, including tales of abductions and mysterious disappearances. These regional variations contribute to the diversity and complexity of the folklore.

6. Influence on Popular Culture:

HAUNTED BY THE JERSEY DEVIL: A JOURNEY INTO AMERICAN FOLKLORE

Stories associating the Jersey Devil with abductions and mysterious disappearances have influenced its portrayal in popular culture, including literature, films, and television. These portrayals have further ingrained the creature's reputation as a formidable and potentially dangerous entity.

Stories of the Jersey Devil being associated with abductions and mysterious disappearances are prevalent within the folklore surrounding the legendary creature. These tales add to the creature's enigmatic and menacing reputation, contributing to its enduring allure and place in American folklore. However, it is important to remember that the Jersey Devil remains a legendary figure, and these stories lack concrete evidence. The creature's impact on popular culture and local traditions continues to captivate the public imagination, inspiring fascination and intrigue for generations to come.

However, it is important to acknowledge that within the realm of folklore and local legends, there have been stories of the Jersey Devil being associated with missing persons. These tales are part of the oral traditions and storytelling that have evolved over time in the Pine Barrens region of New Jersey and its surrounding areas. While not based on factual events, these narratives have contributed to the creature's mystique and the enduring fascination with the legend.

The spread of these narratives can be attributed to several factors:

1. Oral Tradition: The stories of the Jersey Devil's alleged involvement in missing persons cases have been passed down

through generations through oral tradition. Local communities, especially those living in or near the Pine Barrens, have shared these tales during gatherings, family events, and community storytelling sessions.

2. Media and Popular Culture: The Jersey Devil legend and its related stories have been perpetuated through various forms of media and popular culture. Books, newspapers, radio shows, television programs, and later, internet content have all contributed to disseminating the folklore. Fictional works, films, and documentaries inspired by the legend have further cemented its place in popular culture.

3. Local Tourism and Promotion: The legend of the Jersey Devil has become a cultural tourism attraction, particularly in the Pine Barrens area. Local businesses, tour operators, and attractions have capitalized on the creature's popularity, further spreading the legend and its associated narratives.

4. Internet and Social Media: With the advent of the internet and social media, stories about the Jersey Devil and its supposed involvement in missing persons cases have gained wider dissemination. Online forums, websites, and social media platforms have provided a platform for individuals to share and discuss these tales, reaching a broader audience beyond the local communities.

5. Folklore Festivals and Events: Festivals and events celebrating local folklore and legends often include discussions of the Jersey Devil and its stories, perpetuating the narratives and keeping the legend alive.

HAUNTED BY THE JERSEY DEVIL: A JOURNEY INTO AMERICAN FOLKLORE

It is essential to approach these narratives with a critical and discerning mindset, understanding that they are part of a long-standing tradition of storytelling and folklore. While the Jersey Devil remains a captivating and enduring legend, there is no credible evidence linking it to real-life missing persons cases. When it comes to actual missing persons investigations, it is crucial to rely on verified sources and evidence-based information.

Urban legends have a profound psychological impact on communities and individuals within them. These modern folklore narratives thrive on fear, curiosity, and the unknown, tapping into various psychological aspects of human behavior.

Urban legends often prey on people's deepest fears and anxieties. Tales of malevolent entities, dangerous encounters, or inexplicable events evoke a sense of vulnerability and insecurity. Fear can be a compelling emotion, making these stories memorable and likely to be shared among community members as a cautionary tale.

Sharing urban legends fosters social cohesion within communities. When individuals tell these stories, they establish a common ground, creating a shared cultural experience. The act of recounting urban legends strengthens social bonds and promotes a sense of belonging among community members.

The retelling of urban legends offers entertainment and thrill, creating a form of recreational fear. Humans have a fascination with the mysterious and supernatural, and urban legends provide an outlet for exploring these themes in a safe and controlled manner.

Urban legends may serve as a coping mechanism for dealing with real-world fears and uncertainties. By attributing supernatural or paranormal explanations to events, individuals may find comfort in the idea that such occurrences are beyond their control.

Urban legends are transmitted across generations, serving as a form of cultural heritage. Sharing these stories is a way to pass down traditions, values, and beliefs within a community. As a result, urban legends become a part of a community's identity and historical narrative.

Some urban legends carry educational messages or moral lessons. They are often used to caution against certain behaviors or situations, making them a means of informal social guidance.

The psychological impact of urban legends can influence behavior. People may avoid specific locations or activities believed to be linked to these legends, even if the stories are not based on factual events. For example, people may avoid traveling on certain roads or visiting certain sites rumored to be haunted.

Urban legends can also contribute to the spread of rumors and mass hysteria in times of uncertainty or crisis. The sharing of sensational or alarming stories can lead to panic, misinformation, and collective anxiety within a community.

As urban legends are passed down, they can undergo cultural evolution and adaptation, incorporating contemporary elements, technology, or current events. This process ensures their relevance and continued appeal to newer generations.

Urban legends play a significant role in shaping the psychological landscape of communities. They evoke fear, promote social cohesion, and serve as a source of entertainment and cultural heritage. Understanding the psychological aspects of urban legends helps explain why these stories persist and why they continue to captivate and influence people's thoughts and behaviors within their respective communities.

Chapter 9: Exploring Paranormal Explanations

Accounts that attribute paranormal phenomena to the Jersey Devil are prevalent within the folklore and urban legends surrounding the legendary creature. While these accounts lack verifiable evidence, they contribute to the enduring fascination and mystique of the Jersey Devil. Some of the paranormal phenomena attributed to the creature include:

1. Eerie Sounds and Cries: Witnesses have reported hearing eerie sounds and cries emanating from the Pine Barrens, where the Jersey Devil is said to dwell. These sounds are often described as blood-curdling screams, unearthly howls, or the flapping of wings. The haunting nature of these alleged vocalizations adds to the creature's enigmatic presence.

2. Red Glowing Eyes: Many accounts describe the Jersey Devil as having large, red glowing eyes that pierce through the darkness. These glowing eyes are believed to strike fear into those who encounter the creature, adding to its aura of menace.

3. Mysterious Lights: Some sightings of the Jersey Devil involve the observation of mysterious lights moving through the night sky. These lights are often described as glowing orbs or bright flashes, creating an otherworldly ambiance that fuels the legend's supernatural elements.

4. Vanishing and Reappearing Acts: Witnesses have reported seeing the Jersey Devil vanish into thin air or quickly disappear into the dense vegetation of the Pine Barrens. These sudden disappearances contribute to the creature's reputation as an elusive and mysterious entity.

5. Shadowy Apparitions: People have claimed to see shadowy figures or silhouettes resembling the Jersey Devil lurking in the darkness. These fleeting glimpses further perpetuate the legend's element of uncertainty and fear.

6. Apparitions in Mirrors and Reflections: Some legends suggest that the Jersey Devil can be seen in mirrors or reflections, adding a chilling aspect to encounters with the creature. This phenomenon is reminiscent of other supernatural entities from folklore.

7. Haunted Locations: Certain areas in the Pine Barrens are believed to be haunted by the presence of the Jersey Devil. These locations are said to be associated with the creature's past sightings or rumored lair, adding to the region's reputation as a hotbed of paranormal activity.

8. Connection to Other Entities: In some accounts, the Jersey Devil is linked to other paranormal beings or events, such as ghostly apparitions or poltergeist activity. These connections contribute to the creature's association with broader supernatural phenomena.

It is important to reiterate that these accounts are part of the folklore and urban legends surrounding the Jersey Devil, and there is no concrete evidence to support their validity. The folklore and paranormal aspects of the Jersey Devil continue to captivate the public imagination, inspiring curiosity, and further cementing the creature's place in American folklore.

Paranormal investigators and enthusiasts have diverse perspectives on the alleged supernatural abilities of the Jersey Devil. As with any paranormal investigation, beliefs can vary widely, and individuals may hold different interpretations based on their personal experiences, cultural backgrounds, and paranormal theories. Here are some common perspectives among paranormal investigators and enthusiasts regarding the Jersey Devil's alleged supernatural abilities:

1. Open-Minded Approach: Many paranormal investigators and enthusiasts approach the legend of the Jersey Devil with an open mind. They believe that the existence of unknown or unexplained phenomena is possible and are willing to explore various possibilities, including the creature's supernatural abilities.

2. Shape-Shifting and Transformations: Some enthusiasts speculate that the Jersey Devil may possess the ability to shape-shift or transform its appearance. This alleged ability could explain the creature's reported ability to appear differently to different witnesses, adding to the complexity of the folklore.

3. Otherworldly Origin: Some paranormal investigators entertain the idea that the Jersey Devil may not be a natural creature but an entity from another dimension or realm. This perspective aligns with interdimensional or extraterrestrial

theories, suggesting that the creature's abilities are beyond the scope of our known reality.

4. Teleportation and Vanishing Acts: The alleged ability of the Jersey Devil to disappear suddenly or teleport from one location to another intrigues paranormal enthusiasts. They see these accounts as evidence of the creature's paranormal nature, capable of defying conventional laws of physics.

5. Energetic Presence and Negative Energy: Paranormal investigators often associate the Jersey Devil with locations believed to have negative energy or paranormal activity. Some enthusiasts propose that the creature's presence leaves an energetic imprint or influences its surroundings in ways that are beyond normal comprehension.

6. Interactions with Other Entities: Some paranormal investigators explore connections between the Jersey Devil and other supernatural entities or cryptids. They theorize that the creature may be part of a larger, hidden world of unexplained creatures and phenomena.

7. Psychological and Cultural Impact: Beyond the physical manifestations, paranormal enthusiasts also consider the psychological and cultural impact of the Jersey Devil legend. They believe that collective beliefs and emotions can give rise to paranormal experiences and influence people's perceptions of the creature.

8. Scientific Exploration: While some paranormal enthusiasts adopt a more speculative approach, others emphasize the need for scientific investigation. They advocate for empirical

research, data collection, and critical analysis to uncover potential explanations for reported paranormal phenomena associated with the Jersey Devil.

It's important to recognize that while paranormal investigators and enthusiasts explore the legend of the Jersey Devil with genuine curiosity, the evidence supporting the creature's alleged supernatural abilities remains anecdotal and lacking in scientific validation. The perspectives within the paranormal community range from genuine belief to healthy skepticism, and individuals often approach the subject with a mix of fascination and critical thinking. As a result, the legend of the Jersey Devil continues to inspire ongoing discussions and investigations, highlighting the enduring allure of paranormal mysteries within our culture.

The legend of the Jersey Devil blurs the lines between cryptozoology, folklore, and the paranormal, making it a fascinating and complex subject of investigation. Each of these fields explores different aspects of the creature's existence, origins, and cultural significance, leading to a convergence of ideas and perspectives. Let's examine how these disciplines intersect in the context of the Jersey Devil:

1. Cryptozoology:

Cryptozoology is the study of hidden or unknown animals, often focusing on creatures that have not been scientifically proven to exist. In the case of the Jersey Devil, cryptozoologists investigate the possibility of the creature's existence as a yet-to-be-discovered animal species. They explore eyewitness accounts, alleged sightings, and physical evidence (such as footprints and hair samples) to support the idea that the creature might be a real, undiscovered species.

The Jersey Devil's legend fits well within the realm of cryptozoology because it involves reports of a mysterious, elusive, and potentially unique creature. Cryptozoologists attempt to apply scientific methodology to study the evidence and gather data to determine whether the creature is a real biological entity or a product of human imagination and folklore.

2. Folklore:

Folklore refers to the traditional beliefs, customs, and stories passed down within a community or culture. The Jersey Devil legend is deeply rooted in folklore, with multiple variations of the story existing across different New Jersey communities. Folklorists study these narratives, examining how the legend evolves over time, adapts to cultural changes, and is transmitted through oral traditions.

The folklore aspect of the Jersey Devil blurs the lines because, while the legend has its origins in historical accounts, it also incorporates elements of mythology, storytelling, and imaginative embellishment. Over generations, the legend has been shaped by individual storytellers, cultural influences, and local beliefs, making it a dynamic and evolving part of American folklore.

3. The Paranormal:

HAUNTED BY THE JERSEY DEVIL: A JOURNEY INTO AMERICAN FOLKLORE

The paranormal explores phenomena that defy conventional scientific explanation, including ghosts, UFOs, and cryptids like the Jersey Devil. In the context of the Jersey Devil, the paranormal aspect emerges from reports of alleged supernatural abilities attributed to the creature. Witnesses claim to have seen the Jersey Devil vanish into thin air, shape-shift, or exhibit other phenomena that challenge the laws of nature.

These paranormal attributes contribute to the creature's mystique and have led some paranormal investigators to explore the possibility of otherworldly or interdimensional origins. The inclusion of the paranormal perspective introduces an extra layer of complexity to the legend, blending the creature's potential existence in the realm of cryptozoology with its supernatural associations.

The legend of the Jersey Devil blurs the lines between cryptozoology, folklore, and the paranormal, creating a unique and multifaceted subject of interest for researchers, enthusiasts, and the public alike. The interplay between these disciplines enriches the creature's allure and cultural significance, leaving room for exploration, speculation, and ongoing fascination with one of America's most enduring and captivating legends.

Chapter 10: The Jersey Devil in Modern Culture

The legend of the Jersey Devil has inspired numerous portrayals in modern literature, films, and television. Its enduring presence in popular culture showcases the creature's ability to captivate audiences and maintain its status as a cultural icon.

Literature:

1. "The Jersey Devil" by James F. McCloy and Ray Miller Jr.: This book, first published in 1976, offers a comprehensive exploration of the Jersey Devil legend, delving into historical accounts and various interpretations of the creature's existence.

2. "The Last Child" by John Hart: A novel published in 2009, "The Last Child" incorporates the legend of the Jersey Devil into a suspenseful mystery narrative set in the modern-day South.

3. "The Pine Barrens" by John McPhee: This non-fiction book, published in 1967, includes an exploration of the Jersey Devil legend alongside other aspects of the Pine Barrens region and its folklore.

Films:

1. "The 13th Child: Legend of the Jersey Devil" (2002): This horror film follows a group of individuals investigating the

legend of the Jersey Devil and its connection to a series of disappearances.

2. "The Barrens" (2012): In this horror-thriller film, a family camping trip to the Pine Barrens becomes a nightmare when they encounter the Jersey Devil.

3. "The Devil's Tree" (2017): This horror film centers around the legend of a cursed tree in New Jersey that is believed to be the home of the Jersey Devil.

Television:

1. "The X-Files" (Season 4, Episode 5 - "The Field Where I Died"): The popular sci-fi television series featured an episode that briefly explored the Jersey Devil legend as part of its paranormal investigations.

2. "Lost Tapes" (Season 2, Episode 2 - "Jersey Devil"): This found-footage horror mockumentary series presented a fictional encounter with the Jersey Devil, blending elements of folklore and horror.

3. "Supernatural" (Season 9, Episode 13 - "The Purge"): The long-running fantasy-horror series referenced the Jersey Devil in an episode involving a creature responsible for murders in a spa.

These examples demonstrate how the Jersey Devil has been reimagined and incorporated into various genres, from horror and suspense to fantasy and science fiction. The creature's portrayal in modern media has contributed to its continued presence in popular culture, reaching broader audiences and inspiring further interest in its folklore and mystery.

As with any legendary figure, the portrayal of the Jersey Devil in literature, films, and television can vary significantly, ranging from faithful adaptations of the folklore to creative reinterpretations that add new twists and elements to the creature's narrative. The legend's adaptability and enduring appeal ensure that the Jersey Devil remains an enduring subject of exploration and fascination in modern storytelling.

The internet and social media have played a significant role in perpetuating the legend of the Jersey Devil, contributing to its continued popularity and dissemination across a global audience. The digital age has provided a powerful platform for sharing stories, exchanging information, and fostering community engagement, all of which have contributed to the enduring allure of this mythical creature.

1. Increased Accessibility and Visibility: The internet has made information about the Jersey Devil easily accessible to people worldwide. Websites, forums, and online encyclopedias have compiled and organized information about the legend, making it available to anyone with an internet connection. This increased visibility has expanded the creature's reach beyond its local origins.

2. Social Media Sharing: Social media platforms like Facebook, Twitter, Instagram, and Reddit have become hubs for sharing content related to the Jersey Devil. Users can post stories, artwork, photographs, videos, and discussions about sightings,

experiences, and theories, creating a continuous stream of content that keeps the legend alive.

3. User-Generated Content: The internet enables individuals to create and share their own content related to the Jersey Devil. Blogs, vlogs, and websites dedicated to the legend contribute to a vibrant online community where enthusiasts can connect and contribute their own insights and experiences.

4. Viral Content and Memes: The power of viral content and internet memes has further propagated the Jersey Devil legend. Memes, humorous videos, and photoshopped images related to the creature have spread rapidly across social media, reaching wide audiences and cementing the legend's place in online culture.

5. Online Discussions and Forums: Online forums and discussion groups provide spaces for people to exchange stories, theories, and experiences related to the Jersey Devil. These virtual communities foster a sense of belonging and camaraderie among enthusiasts, encouraging further exploration and engagement with the legend.

6. Interactive Platforms: Virtual reality experiences, video games, and online quizzes centered around the Jersey Devil allow users to immerse themselves in the legend and actively participate in the storytelling process.

7. Web Series and Online Documentaries: Creators have produced web series and online documentaries exploring the legend of the Jersey Devil. These digital productions can reach

niche audiences and contribute to ongoing interest in the creature.

8. Crowdsourced Research: The internet has facilitated crowdsourced research on the Jersey Devil. Websites and online databases collect sightings, historical records, and alleged evidence from a wide range of sources, encouraging collaborative investigation and analysis.

While the internet and social media have undoubtedly enhanced the dissemination of the Jersey Devil legend, they have also contributed to a blurring of fact and fiction. The ease of sharing content allows for the rapid spread of hoaxes, fabricated stories, and misinformation, which can influence public perception and contribute to the legend's complexity.

The internet and social media have had a profound influence in perpetuating the legend of the Jersey Devil. These digital platforms provide spaces for storytelling, information exchange, and community building, keeping the folklore alive and relevant in the modern age. However, it is essential to approach online content with critical thinking and discernment, as the lines between reality and imagination can sometimes become blurred in the vast realm of cyberspace.

In contemporary media, the image and mythology of the Jersey Devil have evolved and adapted to suit the tastes and sensibilities of modern audiences. As the legend has become ingrained in popular culture, various media portrayals have reinterpreted the creature's appearance, backstory, and abilities, contributing to its enduring appeal.

In modern media, the Jersey Devil's visual representation has seen significant changes. While historical descriptions often depicted the creature as a horse-like figure with bat-like wings, contemporary portrayals have taken creative liberties to enhance its frightening and fantastical aspects. In films and television shows, the creature is often depicted with a more monstrous and demonic appearance, with elongated limbs, sharp claws, and terrifying eyes, aiming to evoke a sense of horror and awe.

The mythology surrounding the Jersey Devil's origin has also undergone adaptations in contemporary media. While traditional folklore attributes the creature's birth to a woman named Mother Leeds, some modern retellings have introduced alternate origin stories. These variations may involve supernatural events, curses, or experiments gone awry, adding complexity and depth to the creature's backstory.

In contemporary media, the Jersey Devil is sometimes portrayed as a multidimensional character with motives, emotions, and complexities. Some stories explore the creature's perspective, giving it depth beyond the role of a mere antagonist. This approach humanizes the creature to some extent, allowing audiences to empathize with or understand its actions, even if they are ultimately malevolent.

The Jersey Devil has become a cultural icon and appears in various forms of media beyond traditional storytelling. It is often referenced or incorporated into popular culture through merchandise, video games, internet memes, and artwork, contributing to its ongoing presence in modern society.

HAUNTED BY THE JERSEY DEVIL: A JOURNEY INTO AMERICAN FOLKLORE

The creature's mythology has transcended traditional media, appearing in diverse formats. For example, web series, podcasts, and interactive storytelling experiences have further expanded the legend's reach, attracting new audiences and providing fresh perspectives on the folklore.

Some modern portrayals of the Jersey Devil subvert traditional folklore and genre conventions. Creators blend horror with comedy, fantasy, or science fiction elements, creating unique and unexpected narratives that challenge conventional storytelling norms.

Contemporary media portrayals often use the Jersey Devil legend as a vehicle to explore deeper themes and messages. These themes may include environmental conservation, the consequences of human actions, the impact of urban legends on communities, and the complexities of belief and skepticism.

Overall, the evolution of the Jersey Devil's image and mythology in contemporary media reflects the creature's enduring popularity and adaptability as a storytelling trope. The various interpretations and creative adaptations keep the legend fresh and relevant, allowing it to continue captivating audiences across different generations and cultural contexts. The creature's journey through modern media ensures that the Jersey Devil remains a compelling and ever-evolving figure in the realm of folklore and popular culture.

Chapter 11: Psychological and Sociological Aspects

———

Belief in mythical creatures like the Jersey Devil is influenced by a combination of psychological factors that shape human cognition, perception, and cultural context. These factors contribute to the enduring fascination with such creatures and the willingness of individuals to accept their existence despite the lack of concrete evidence. Some key psychological factors behind belief in mythical creatures include:

1. Imagination and Storytelling: Humans have a natural inclination towards imagination and storytelling. Mythical creatures like the Jersey Devil are born from creative minds, passed down through generations via oral traditions, written accounts, and contemporary media. The power of storytelling allows these creatures to be vividly depicted in the minds of believers, contributing to a sense of realism and emotional connection.

2. Fear and Uncertainty: Fear is a fundamental emotion that has evolutionary significance for survival. Belief in mythical creatures often stems from fears of the unknown, darkness, and dangerous landscapes. These creatures embody those fears, making them cautionary tales that remind people of potential dangers in their environment.

3. Pattern Recognition and Pareidolia: The human brain is wired to recognize patterns and shapes, even in random or ambiguous stimuli. In environments like the dense woods of the Pine Barrens, where the Jersey Devil is said to dwell, our brains may interpret shadows, sounds, or glimpses of wildlife as evidence of a mythical creature.

4. Cultural Conditioning: Cultural beliefs and traditions strongly influence beliefs in mythical creatures. Growing up in a culture that embraces folklore and legends may lead individuals to accept these stories as part of their cultural heritage. Exposure to local tales and community beliefs further reinforces the acceptance of such creatures as real.

5. Social Influence and Conformity: Belief in mythical creatures can be reinforced by social influence and conformity within a community. When a significant number of people in a community believe in the existence of a creature like the Jersey Devil, it creates a social norm that encourages others to adopt similar beliefs.

6. Coping Mechanisms and Symbolism: Belief in mythical creatures can serve as coping mechanisms for dealing with real-world uncertainties and anxieties. These creatures can symbolize broader fears and conflicts, providing a way for individuals to grapple with complex emotions and experiences.

7. Desire for Mystery and Wonder: Humans are drawn to mysteries and the unknown. Believing in mythical creatures like the Jersey Devil can provide a sense of wonder and

excitement, sparking curiosity and imagination about the unexplained aspects of the world.

8. Personal Experiences and Anecdotal Evidence: Personal experiences and anecdotal evidence, while not scientifically valid, can have a profound impact on belief. When individuals claim to have encountered a creature or experienced unexplained events, it can reinforce the belief in the creature's existence, especially within close-knit communities.

It is essential to recognize that belief in mythical creatures does not rely on empirical evidence but rather on a complex interplay of psychological factors. While some individuals may hold genuine beliefs in the Jersey Devil and other mythical creatures, others may appreciate them as cultural heritage, storytelling devices, or symbolic representations of human experiences. The psychological factors behind belief in these creatures contribute to the rich tapestry of human culture and the enduring allure of the unknown.

The role of cultural identity and community beliefs is pivotal in shaping the longevity of the legend of the Jersey Devil. The legend's enduring presence can be attributed to how it resonates with the cultural identity of the communities where it originated and how it continues to be passed down through generations. Several factors contribute to the legend's longevity through cultural identity and community beliefs:

1. Oral Tradition: The Jersey Devil legend thrives through oral tradition, passed down from one generation to another within local communities. Through storytelling, the legend becomes

an integral part of the community's cultural heritage, connecting individuals with their ancestors and shared history.

2. Sense of Belonging: Embracing the Jersey Devil legend fosters a sense of belonging and collective identity among community members. The legend becomes a unifying force that binds people together, creating a shared cultural experience that reinforces social bonds.

3. Reinforcement of Local Identity: The legend is often tied to specific geographic locations, such as the Pine Barrens of New Jersey. Embracing the Jersey Devil as part of local folklore reinforces the distinct identity of these communities and enhances their uniqueness within a broader cultural context.

4. Rituals and Festivals: Local festivals, celebrations, and rituals centered around the Jersey Devil contribute to the legend's longevity. These events reinforce the cultural significance of the creature and its importance within the community's traditions.

5. Education and Family Influence: Within families and communities, elders often play a crucial role in passing down the legend to younger generations. The belief in the Jersey Devil becomes a rite of passage and a way to impart cultural values and knowledge from one generation to the next.

6. Shared History and Experiences: The Jersey Devil legend can be intertwined with historical events and experiences shared by the community. Whether as an allegory for past hardships or as a source of local pride, the legend becomes deeply ingrained in the collective memory of the community.

7. Cultural Resilience: The continued belief in the Jersey Devil reflects the resilience of cultural traditions and beliefs, especially in the face of external influences and modernization. Embracing the legend helps communities maintain a connection with their past and preserve their unique cultural identity.

8. Tourism and Local Economy: For regions like the Pine Barrens, the Jersey Devil legend has economic implications. It serves as a cultural tourism attraction, drawing visitors who are eager to explore the legend's history and associated sites. This sustains interest in the legend and contributes to its longevity.

Overall, cultural identity and community beliefs play a significant role in shaping the legend of the Jersey Devil's longevity. The legend is more than just a tale; it becomes a vital aspect of the community's shared history, values, and sense of self. Through storytelling, rituals, and intergenerational transmission, the belief in the Jersey Devil continues to thrive, ensuring its place in the cultural fabric of the communities that cherish and perpetuate it.

The legend of the Jerscy Devil has had a significant impact on local tourism in the Pine Barrens region of New Jersey, where the creature is said to reside. As a cultural and economic resource, the legend attracts visitors from near and far, boosting tourism-related activities and contributing to the local economy. Here are some key aspects of the legend's impact on tourism and its use as a cultural and economic resource:

1. Cultural Tourism: The Jersey Devil legend has become a cultural tourism attraction in the Pine Barrens. Tourists are drawn to the region to explore the folklore, learn about the legend's history, and visit sites associated with alleged sightings or the creature's supposed lair. Guided tours, museums, and historical markers provide visitors with opportunities to immerse themselves in the legend's rich cultural heritage.

2. Festivals and Events: Local festivals and events centered around the Jersey Devil contribute to tourism and community engagement. These events celebrate the legend's cultural significance and attract visitors seeking unique experiences, entertainment, and the chance to participate in the folklore-inspired festivities.

3. Souvenirs and Merchandise: The popularity of the Jersey Devil legend has led to the creation of a wide range of souvenirs and merchandise, including t-shirts, books, keychains, and artwork. Tourists often purchase these items as mementos of their visit, further boosting the local economy and promoting the legend.

4. Hospitality Industry: The legend's influence on tourism has a positive impact on the local hospitality industry. Hotels, motels, restaurants, and other accommodations benefit from the influx of tourists seeking to explore the legend and surrounding attractions.

5. Supporting Local Businesses: The legend's status as a cultural and economic resource extends beyond the immediate tourist attractions. Local businesses, such as eateries, gift shops, and

transportation services, benefit from increased patronage as a result of tourism generated by the Jersey Devil legend.

6. Art and Entertainment: The legend's cultural significance has inspired local artists, writers, and filmmakers, who create works that draw on the folklore and enhance the region's creative output. This artistic expression further contributes to the legend's appeal and its portrayal in contemporary media.

7. Educational and Research Opportunities: Tourism related to the Jersey Devil legend also creates opportunities for educational initiatives and research. Local organizations and academic institutions may conduct studies, host lectures, or offer educational programs to explore the folklore's historical, cultural, and sociological aspects.

8. Economic Diversification: For regions heavily reliant on a specific industry, such as agriculture or manufacturing, the Jersey Devil legend can offer economic diversification. Tourism revenue helps balance the local economy and provides an alternative income stream.

It is essential to balance the promotion of the legend as a cultural and economic resource with responsible stewardship of the region's natural environment and historical sites. Sustainable tourism practices can ensure the preservation of the Pine Barrens' unique landscapes and heritage while fostering a respectful and educational experience for visitors.

The legend of the Jersey Devil serves as a valuable cultural and economic resource for the Pine Barrens region. Its impact on local tourism attracts visitors, supports businesses, and celebrates the area's cultural heritage. As a result, the legend continues to thrive, sustaining interest in the folklore, and contributing to the economic vitality of the communities that embrace it.

Chapter 12: Cryptids and Cryptotourism

The global fascination with cryptids, which are creatures that are rumored to exist but lack concrete scientific evidence, can be attributed to several factors that resonate with human curiosity, imagination, and cultural symbolism. Cryptids have become cultural symbols due to their ability to tap into universal themes, evoke emotions, and embody shared values and fears. Here are some reasons why cryptids capture the imagination and become cultural symbols:

1. Mystery and the Unknown: Cryptids represent the unknown, the mysterious, and the unexplained. Humans have an innate fascination with the uncharted territories of the natural world, and cryptids embody this sense of wonder and curiosity. They become symbols of the hidden and the undiscovered, sparking the desire to explore and uncover hidden truths.

2. Mythology and Folklore: Many cryptids have their origins in ancient mythology and local folklore. These legends are deeply ingrained in cultural narratives and serve as a means of passing down knowledge, values, and beliefs from one generation to the next. Cryptids, as part of folklore, carry cultural significance and become symbols of cultural identity and heritage.

3. Connection to Nature and the Environment: Cryptids are often associated with specific geographical regions, wildlife habitats, or ecological niches. They serve as symbols of the environment's fragility and the need for conservation efforts. As cultural symbols, cryptids may inspire people to protect natural habitats and wildlife.

4. Fear and Thrill: Cryptids often evoke fear and excitement. Stories of encounters with these elusive creatures tap into primal emotions, such as fear of the unknown and the thrill of danger. As cultural symbols, cryptids become vessels for exploring human emotions and the boundaries of our understanding.

5. Symbolism of the Unseen: Cryptids represent the boundary between reality and the imagination. As cultural symbols, they embody the unseen forces and mysteries that shape our lives, making them vehicles for exploring abstract concepts and the intangible aspects of the human experience.

6. Folk Heroes and Antiheroes: Some cryptids, like Bigfoot or the Loch Ness Monster, are portrayed as folk heroes or antiheroes in popular culture. They become symbols of rebellion, defiance against authority, or representations of misunderstood beings.

7. Counter Culture and Subversion: Cryptids often have a place in counter-culture and subversive movements. They challenge mainstream scientific and societal norms, becoming symbols of resistance to dominant narratives and established institutions.

8. Entertainment and Fantasy: Cryptids have become icons of the fantasy genre, appearing in literature, films, video games, and other forms of media. Their fantastical nature adds to their appeal as cultural symbols that transport people to imaginative realms.

Overall, the global fascination with cryptids stems from their ability to evoke wonder, fear, and imagination. As cultural symbols, they serve as mirrors of the human psyche, reflecting our desires, fears, and the yearning for exploration and understanding. Cryptids have become part of our shared cultural lexicon, enriching the diverse tapestry of global folklore and shaping how we perceive the unknown and the enigmatic aspects of the natural world.

Cryptotourism, also known as monster tourism or cryptid tourism, refers to a niche form of travel where individuals visit locations associated with mythical creatures, legends, and cryptids. The rise of cryptotourism has been fueled by the global fascination with mysterious creatures like the Jersey Devil, drawing curious travelers to destinations with rich folklore and tales of legendary beings.

New Jersey, specifically the Pine Barrens region, has embraced the legend of the Jersey Devil, leveraging its cultural significance to attract tourists from around the world. Here's how the Jersey Devil draws visitors to New Jersey:

1. Cultural Attraction: The legend of the Jersey Devil has become an integral part of New Jersey's cultural heritage, particularly in the Pine Barrens region. Tourists are drawn to

explore the folklore, learn about local traditions, and immerse themselves in the unique cultural experience that the legend provides.

2. Myth and Mystery: Cryptotourists seek out locations that offer a sense of mystery and adventure. The Jersey Devil, as a cryptid with a long-standing legend, perfectly fits this desire for the unknown. Visitors are intrigued by the enigmatic creature and the possibility of encountering a living myth.

3. Festivals and Events: New Jersey hosts festivals and events dedicated to the Jersey Devil legend, such as the "Annual Legend of the Jersey Devil" festival and "Jersey Devil Hunt" events. These gatherings attract cryptotourists who want to be part of the celebrations and immerse themselves in the legend's atmosphere.

4. Guided Tours and Merchandise: The tourism industry capitalizes on the Jersey Devil's popularity by offering guided tours through the Pine Barrens, showcasing sites associated with the legend. Additionally, merchandise, including t-shirts, keychains, and books, provides tourists with souvenirs to commemorate their experience.

5. Social Media and Internet Presence: The rise of social media and the internet has played a significant role in promoting cryptotourism. Online platforms allow enthusiasts to share stories, sightings, and experiences related to the Jersey Devil, creating a virtual community that amplifies the legend's allure and reaches a global audience.

6. Cryptid-Conventions: Cryptid conventions and conferences have gained popularity among enthusiasts, and the Jersey Devil often features as a central theme in these gatherings. Such events attract a diverse group of attendees, including researchers, believers, skeptics, and curious travelers.

7. Educational and Paranormal Interest: Some tourists are drawn to the Jersey Devil legend due to their interest in the paranormal and unexplained phenomena. The creature's association with supernatural abilities and mysterious sightings appeals to those seeking an educational and immersive experience.

8. Economic Impact: Cryptotourism contributes to the local economy, boosting revenue for businesses in the region. Hotels, restaurants, tour operators, and local vendors benefit from the influx of tourists interested in exploring the legend of the Jersey Devil.

The rise of cryptotourism has seen an increasing number of travelers seeking out destinations with connections to mythical creatures and legends. The Jersey Devil, as a prominent figure in American folklore, serves as a potent draw for tourists to New Jersey's Pine Barrens. The legend's cultural significance, combined with the sense of mystery and adventure it offers, continues to attract visitors, sustaining interest in the creature and contributing to the region's tourism industry.

Promoting cryptids for tourism purposes raises several ethical considerations that need careful examination. While cryptotourism can generate economic benefits for local communities and support cultural heritage, it must be balanced with ethical responsibilities to the environment, local culture, and the promotion of responsible tourism practices. Here are some key ethical considerations:

1. Conservation and Environmental Impact: Cryptotourism can increase foot traffic in natural habitats, potentially disturbing local wildlife and ecosystems. It is crucial to ensure that tourism activities are managed responsibly, with a focus on preserving the environment and minimizing negative impacts on wildlife and sensitive ecosystems.

2. Cultural Sensitivity: The promotion of cryptids for tourism purposes should respect the cultural beliefs and traditions of local communities. It is essential to avoid exploitation or misrepresentation of folklore and cultural heritage for commercial gain. Instead, emphasis should be placed on sharing cultural stories with respect and accuracy.

3. Misleading Tourist Expectations: Promoting cryptids for tourism can create unrealistic expectations among visitors, who may anticipate encounters with mythical creatures or supernatural experiences. Responsible marketing and education are essential to manage these expectations and prevent disappointment or deception.

4. Responsible Research and Documentation: Ethical considerations should prioritize responsible research and documentation of cryptids. Misleading or exaggerated claims about the existence of mythical creatures can undermine scientific credibility and perpetuate misinformation.

5. Protecting Wildlife and Habitats: While promoting cryptids, it is essential to prioritize the conservation of existing wildlife and their habitats. Activities should not encourage or facilitate the exploitation of natural resources or endanger species for the sake of attracting tourists.

6. Respect for Local Communities: Cryptotourism can impact the daily lives of local communities, leading to changes in cultural practices and increased pressure on resources. Sustainable tourism practices should respect the rights and customs of local residents and involve them in decision-making processes.

7. Balancing Cultural Heritage and Commercialization: Finding a balance between preserving cultural heritage and commercialization is crucial. While promoting cryptids may enhance tourism, it is essential not to commodify sacred or sensitive aspects of local culture.

8. Mitigating Harmful Behaviors: Ethical considerations should address potential harmful behaviors associated with cryptotourism, such as trespassing, vandalism, or disruptive activities in natural habitats. Responsible tourism guidelines should be established to mitigate these negative impacts.

9. Encouraging Education and Awareness: Cryptotourism can be an opportunity to promote education and awareness about the cultural significance of cryptids and their role in folklore. By focusing on educational components, tourists can gain a deeper understanding and appreciation for the legends while supporting local culture.

Promoting cryptids for tourism purposes presents both opportunities and ethical challenges. Striking a balance between economic benefits, cultural preservation, and responsible environmental practices is essential to ensure that cryptotourism contributes positively to local communities and respects the integrity of the environment and cultural heritage. Ethical considerations should guide the development of sustainable and respectful tourism practices, creating a meaningful and responsible experience for both tourists and local residents.

HAUNTED BY THE JERSEY DEVIL: A JOURNEY INTO AMERICAN FOLKLORE

Chapter 13: Theories of Origin

The legend of the Jersey Devil has sparked various theories attempting to explain its origins. As with many folklore and cryptid tales, these theories range from historical events and misidentifications to psychological and sociological interpretations.

One theory suggests that the Jersey Devil legend originated from historical events and political satire during the 18th century. The legend is believed to be a combination of stories about a deformed child born to a local woman, Mother Leeds, and political cartoons lampooning Daniel Leeds, a prominent Quaker and almanac publisher. It is suggested that the legend served as a form of political commentary and satire, mocking the Leeds family and their beliefs.

Another theory posits that the Jersey Devil legend is based on sightings of prehistoric creatures or pterosaurs that may have survived into modern times. Proponents of this theory suggest that people in the region may have encountered unknown species of animals, which they interpreted as the mythical creature.

Some theories suggest that the Jersey Devil legend is a result of cultural borrowing from European folklore. Similar creatures, such as the Leeds Devil or L Leeds, were part of English and German legends. When settlers from these regions arrived in America, they may have brought their folklore with them and adapted it to the local landscape, giving rise to the Jersey Devil legend.

Environmental factors may have contributed to the legend's origin. The Pine Barrens, the region associated with the Jersey Devil, is a harsh and desolate landscape, which might have led to stress and anxiety among early settlers. This stress, coupled with a strong tradition of storytelling and imagination, may have given birth to the legend as a way to explain the unknown and the dangers of the wilderness.

There are theories suggesting that the Jersey Devil sightings were the result of hoaxes and pranks perpetuated by locals or outsiders to create fear and excitement. In some cases, these hoaxes may have been for personal amusement, while in others, they could have been used to attract attention or promote tourism in the region.

The legend's persistence could be attributed to social and cultural dynamics. As the legend became embedded in local folklore and tradition, it was passed down through generations, solidifying its presence in the community's collective memory. Additionally, the legend's popularity could have been reinforced by factors such as social conformity and the desire to preserve cultural heritage.

It is important to note that while these theories offer potential explanations for the origins of the Jersey Devil legend, the true source of the tale remains uncertain. Folklore and legends often evolve through a combination of historical events, cultural influences, and human imagination, making it challenging to pinpoint a definitive origin. The enduring allure of the Jersey Devil legend lies in its ability to capture the human imagination and persist as an enduring enigma in American folklore.

The legend of the Jersey Devil has deep historical roots that are intertwined with Native American influences, historical events, and religious beliefs. While the exact origins of the legend remain elusive, these factors have likely played significant roles in shaping the creature's creation and subsequent evolution.

The Pine Barrens region of New Jersey, where the Jersey Devil legend is centered, was historically inhabited by several Native American tribes, including the Lenape (also known as the Delaware Indians). Native American folklore and beliefs about supernatural beings and mythical creatures may have contributed to the genesis of the legend.

Tales of "shape-shifters" and trickster spirits, common in Native American folklore, could have influenced the concept of a creature with a human-like form but supernatural abilities. Additionally, Native American tribes often have their own stories about fearsome beings or cryptids associated with specific geographical locations, which could have contributed to the legend's cultural context.

The early European settlers in the Pine Barrens faced numerous challenges, including harsh environmental conditions, isolation, and potential conflicts with Native American tribes. Historical events, such as reports of animal attacks, livestock predation, and unexplained occurrences, might have fueled fears and contributed to the creation of a creature that embodied these anxieties.

Religion and superstition played influential roles in the lives of early settlers. The belief in the supernatural, the devil, and malevolent entities was prevalent in European cultures of the time. The legend of the Jersey Devil could have emerged as a way to personify these fears and explain unexplained phenomena in a religious and moral context.

The legend of the Jersey Devil gained significant popularity in the 19th century, a time when Gothic literature and folklore were thriving. The rise of newspapers and increased literacy also facilitated the dissemination of stories and contributed to the spread of the legend to a broader audience.

European settlers in the region may have brought with them their own folktales and legends, which were then adapted to fit the local landscape and culture. This cultural borrowing and adaptation could have resulted in the synthesis of different elements to create the legend of the Jersey Devil.

As mentioned earlier, the legend of the Jersey Devil may have been influenced by political and social commentary, with certain elements serving as satirical representations of prominent figures or events.

It is essential to recognize that the creation and evolution of folklore and legends like the Jersey Devil are complex and multifaceted processes. Multiple influences, historical events, and cultural beliefs interact to shape these narratives over time.

As a result, the legend of the Jersey Devil represents not only a specific mythical creature but also a reflection of the fears, beliefs, and cultural dynamics of the communities that have preserved and perpetuated it throughout history.

The origin theories surrounding the legend of the Jersey Devil reflect the cultural anxieties and hopes of different time periods, providing insight into the fears, aspirations, and concerns that shaped the narrative over centuries. The evolution of the legend can be seen as a reflection of the changing cultural context and the socio-historical factors influencing the beliefs and values of the communities involved.

Incorporating Native American influences into the legend reflects a cultural anxiety about the unknown and the supernatural. Native American folklore often includes stories of shape-shifters, spirits, and mythical creatures, mirroring a deep connection to the natural world and the mysteries it holds. Early European settlers in the 17th and 18th centuries may have been anxious about their unfamiliar surroundings and the potential encounters with the unfamiliar Native American beliefs, contributing to the assimilation of Native American elements into the legend.

During times of hardship and uncertainty, cultural anxieties tend to surface in legends and folklore. Reports of animal attacks, livestock predation, and unexplained occurrences could have amplified the settlers' fears about the dangers of the wilderness and their vulnerability in a new and isolated environment. Creating a creature like the Jersey Devil provided an outlet to personify these fears and attribute them to a malevolent entity.

Religious and superstitious beliefs have long been influential factors in shaping folklore and legends. In the 18th and 19th centuries, Christian beliefs in the devil and malevolent forces were widespread, and the legend of the Jersey Devil tapped into these religious anxieties. The creature's association with the devil reflected the cultural fears of sin, punishment, and moral corruption.

The rise of Gothic literature and the fascination with supernatural themes in the 19th century influenced the portrayal of mythical creatures and cryptids. The popularity of Gothic novels like "Frankenstein" and "Dracula" mirrored a cultural fascination with the mysterious and macabre, contributing to the appeal of the Jersey Devil legend during that period.

Cultural borrowing and adaptation reflect a hope for continuity and a desire to preserve cultural identity. By incorporating elements from European folklore and adapting them to the local landscape, settlers reinforced their cultural heritage while simultaneously establishing a unique and distinct legend for their new environment.

Using the legend as a form of political and social commentary reflects a hope for change or resistance against authority. During times of political unrest or social upheaval, satire and political cartoons were common forms of expression. The Jersey Devil legend, as a satirical representation of figures like

Daniel Leeds, expressed dissatisfaction with the political climate and the desire for social change.

The origin theories of the Jersey Devil legend provide valuable insights into the cultural anxieties and hopes of different time periods. From fears of the unknown and the supernatural to hopes for cultural continuity and social change, the legend reflects the complexities of human emotions and the dynamic interplay between cultural beliefs and historical events. As a result, the legend of the Jersey Devil continues to be a rich and enduring reflection of the cultural heritage and aspirations of the communities that have nurtured and adapted it throughout history.

Chapter 14: The Search for Physical Evidence

Attempts to find physical evidence or remains of the Jersey Devil have been ongoing for many years, but to date, no concrete evidence supporting the creature's existence has been discovered. Numerous expeditions, investigations, and searches have been conducted in the Pine Barrens and other areas associated with the legend, but they have not yielded any conclusive evidence. Here are some of the notable attempts made to find evidence of the Jersey Devil:

1. Sightings and Witness Accounts: Many eyewitnesses have claimed to have seen the Jersey Devil over the years. These alleged sightings have led to searches in specific locations where the creature was reportedly spotted. However, the accounts are often inconsistent and lack verifiable evidence.

2. Scientific Investigations: Some researchers have conducted scientific studies and investigations in the Pine Barrens, employing techniques like wildlife monitoring, night vision cameras, and audio recording to detect any potential unknown creatures. Yet, these efforts have not provided definitive evidence of the Jersey Devil's existence.

3. Cryptozoological Expeditions: Cryptid enthusiasts and investigators have organized expeditions and research efforts in hopes of capturing evidence of the Jersey Devil. These expeditions often involve interviews with witnesses,

exploration of the region, and deployment of specialized equipment, but they have not resulted in any tangible proof.

4. Rewards and Incentives: Over the years, rewards have been offered to anyone who can provide substantial evidence or capture the Jersey Devil. Despite the incentives, no verifiable evidence has been presented.

5. Skeptical Perspectives: Skeptics have also analyzed the claims and evidence related to the Jersey Devil, pointing out logical fallacies, misidentifications, and the lack of credible evidence. They argue that the legend is a product of folklore, superstition, and sensationalism rather than a real creature.

6. Hoaxes and Pranks: Some attempts to find the Jersey Devil have been thwarted by hoaxes and pranks. Individuals seeking attention or amusement have staged sightings or created fake evidence, further complicating genuine research efforts.

Despite the lack of physical evidence, the legend of the Jersey Devil continues to captivate the public imagination and remains an essential part of American folklore. While the search for the creature's existence persists, it is crucial to approach the subject with a scientific and critical mindset, acknowledging the lack of substantiated evidence while respecting the cultural significance and historical context of the legend.

The history of reported findings related to the Jersey Devil includes alleged tracks, carcasses, and other pieces of evidence that have been presented as potential proof of the creature's existence. However, it is essential to approach these claims with a critical mindset, as the authenticity of many of these findings remains questionable.

Numerous reports of footprints and tracks attributed to the Jersey Devil have surfaced over the years. These tracks are often described as having a horseshoe-like shape with claw-like impressions. One of the earliest documented instances of tracks was in January 1909 when a series of strange footprints were found in the snow in various locations in New Jersey and Pennsylvania. The tracks were dubbed "Jersey Devil tracks" by the media, adding to the legend's intrigue.

In more recent times, some individuals have claimed to find tracks in the Pine Barrens region and surrounding areas, but these findings have not been scientifically verified. Critics argue that many of these tracks can be attributed to other animals or natural causes, such as misidentified tracks from common wildlife like deer, dogs, or birds.

There have been instances of alleged Jersey Devil carcasses being discovered. For example, in 1957, a farmer claimed to have found a strange creature that resembled the Jersey Devil on his property in New Jersey. However, upon examination, it was determined to be the remains of a decomposed raccoon with its legs spread wide apart, creating an illusion of a larger creature.

Similarly, in the late 19th century, a reward was offered for the capture of the Jersey Devil, leading some individuals to present carcasses, which were later revealed to be hoaxes or misidentified animal remains.

Various artifacts and pieces of evidence have been presented over the years to support the legend of the Jersey Devil. These include photographs, drawings, and alleged eyewitness accounts. However, the authenticity and reliability of such evidence have often been called into question due to lack of corroborating evidence or verifiable sources.

Skeptics and researchers have scrutinized many of these reported findings and have often been able to debunk them. Skeptics argue that the legend of the Jersey Devil is primarily a product of folklore, urban legends, and sensationalism rather than actual physical evidence of a real creature.

While there have been numerous reported findings related to the Jersey Devil over the years, most of them lack concrete scientific evidence and can be explained by natural causes, misidentifications, or hoaxes. As a result, the mystery of the Jersey Devil's existence persists, and the legend continues to be a captivating and enduring part of American folklore.

Experts in paleontology and zoology can offer valuable insights into the feasibility of discovering evidence for the existence of the Jersey Devil or any cryptid. These experts rely on scientific methodologies and knowledge of animal behavior, evolution, and ecological systems to assess the likelihood of finding evidence for purported mythical creatures. Here are some key points they would consider:

1. Lack of Fossil Records: Paleontologists study the fossil records to understand the history of life on Earth. The absence of any fossil evidence or remains resembling the Jersey Devil

raises doubts about its existence as a biological entity. Given the extensive research on prehistoric animals and their evolution, the lack of any known fossils or related genetic evidence of a cryptid like the Jersey Devil casts doubt on its feasibility.

2. Biodiversity and Ecological Considerations: Zoologists study the diversity of life forms and their interactions within ecosystems. They assess the likelihood of a new species or cryptid surviving and thriving in a specific environment. In the case of the Jersey Devil, the Pine Barrens' ecosystem has been extensively studied, and no evidence of an unknown apex predator or cryptid has been found, suggesting that it is highly improbable.

3. Lack of Supporting Ecological Niche: Zoologists consider the ecological niche that a creature would need to occupy within its environment to survive. For a large, winged creature like the Jersey Devil to exist, it would require significant resources and a suitable ecological niche to sustain its population. The Pine Barrens region is well-researched, and no such niche that could support a large, unknown predator has been identified.

4. Behavioral and Habitat Research: Experts in animal behavior and ecology would consider the lifestyle and habitat requirements of the Jersey Devil as described in folklore. They would analyze if such a creature's behavior and habitat preferences align with known animal behaviors and ecological niches. Based on the creature's described characteristics, the

feasibility of its survival in the known environment would be evaluated.

5. Sightings and Witness Accounts: While eyewitness accounts can be valuable in generating leads, experts emphasize the importance of critical analysis. Zoologists and paleontologists would scrutinize the reliability and consistency of the accounts and assess the potential for misidentifications, hoaxes, or exaggerations.

Experts in paleontology and zoology approach claims of mythical creatures like the Jersey Devil with skepticism due to the lack of concrete evidence, inconsistent witness accounts, and the extensive knowledge of known animal species and ecological systems. While they acknowledge the importance of cultural and folklore studies, their scientific training leads them to seek empirical evidence and critical analysis in evaluating the feasibility of discovering evidence for such creatures. Until verifiable scientific evidence emerges, the Jersey Devil remains a captivating part of folklore rather than a confirmed biological entity.

HAUNTED BY THE JERSEY DEVIL: A JOURNEY INTO AMERICAN FOLKLORE

Chapter 15: Cryptozoology and Conservation

The role of cryptozoology in conservation efforts for mythical creatures like the Jersey Devil is a subject of debate within the scientific and conservation communities. Cryptozoology is the study of hidden or unknown animals, often focusing on creatures with limited or disputed scientific evidence. While some proponents argue that cryptozoology can contribute to conservation efforts, others criticize it as diverting attention and resources away from more pressing conservation priorities. Let's explore both perspectives:

Proponents of Cryptozoology in Conservation Efforts:

1. RAISING AWARENESS: Cryptozoology can generate public interest and curiosity about mythical creatures, including the Jersey Devil. This heightened awareness can lead to discussions about the importance of wildlife conservation and the need to protect biodiversity, even if the specific creature in question is not scientifically validated.

2. Supporting Ecosystem Conservation: The study of mythical creatures often involves exploration of remote or lesser-known ecosystems. These expeditions can provide valuable data about the habitat, flora, and fauna of these regions, potentially leading to discoveries of new species or ecological insights.

3. Preserving Cultural Heritage: Embracing mythical creatures as cultural symbols can promote the preservation of cultural heritage and indigenous knowledge. By engaging with local communities and their folklore, conservationists can foster a sense of stewardship for the natural environment and its inhabitants.

4. Ecotourism Potential: Interest in mythical creatures can attract eco-tourists to specific regions, providing economic incentives for communities to protect their natural resources and promote sustainable practices.

Critics of Cryptozoology in Conservation Efforts:

1. DIVERSION OF RESOURCES: Critics argue that resources and attention directed towards the investigation of mythical creatures could be better utilized for research on real and threatened species facing extinction.

2. Scientific Credibility: Cryptozoology's focus on creatures without substantial scientific evidence can undermine the credibility of the broader conservation field. This may result in skepticism and reluctance to support genuine conservation efforts.

3. Ethical Concerns: Engaging in expeditions or investigations without adequate scientific evidence can raise ethical concerns, particularly if they involve disrupting habitats or exploiting local communities for sensationalist purposes.

4. Misuse of Conservation Funds: Allocating funds for cryptozoological research could be seen as wasteful or misdirected, especially when there are pressing conservation needs that require financial support.

The role of cryptozoology in conservation efforts for mythical creatures like the Jersey Devil is complex and contentious. While it can raise awareness, promote cultural preservation, and contribute to scientific knowledge about certain ecosystems, it also faces criticism for diverting resources from more established and pressing conservation priorities. Striking a balance between fostering interest in wildlife and ecosystem preservation while adhering to scientific rigor is essential to ensure that cryptozoology can play a constructive role in conservation efforts.

The legend of the Jersey Devil can inspire interest in protecting the natural habitats of the Pine Barrens in several ways:

1. CULTURAL SIGNIFICANCE: The legend of the Jersey Devil is deeply rooted in the cultural heritage of the region. By associating the creature with the Pine Barrens, the legend highlights the importance of preserving this unique and ecologically diverse area. The tale serves as a symbol of the region's identity, drawing attention to its natural beauty and ecological significance.

2. Ecotourism and Conservation Awareness: The popularity of the Jersey Devil legend attracts visitors to the Pine Barrens, fostering ecotourism opportunities. Ecotourists interested in

exploring the legend's origins and the natural landscapes associated with it may gain a deeper appreciation for the region's ecological importance. This heightened interest can lead to greater awareness of the need to protect the Pine Barrens and its habitats.

3. Conservation Education: The legend provides an opportunity to engage the public in conservation education. Local conservation organizations and park authorities can use the legend as a starting point to introduce visitors to the unique flora and fauna of the Pine Barrens. Interpretive centers and guided tours can focus on the region's biodiversity and the significance of conserving this natural treasure.

4. Ecosystem Protection: The legend of the Jersey Devil can be a gateway to discussions about the delicate balance of ecosystems and the potential threats they face. Emphasizing the interdependence of species and the ecological role of the Pine Barrens helps underscore the importance of preserving this habitat.

5. Habitat Restoration Efforts: Interest in the legend can mobilize conservation groups to undertake habitat restoration initiatives within the Pine Barrens. When people connect emotionally with a place through folklore and legends, they are more likely to engage in active conservation efforts to protect it.

6. Sustainable Development: The legend's popularity can encourage communities and local authorities to prioritize sustainable development practices. By recognizing the value

of the Pine Barrens as a natural attraction, stakeholders may work towards balancing economic growth with ecological preservation.

7. Research and Scientific Study: As the legend continues to captivate the public, it can attract researchers and scientists to study the Pine Barrens and its wildlife. This influx of scientific interest can contribute to a better understanding of the region's biodiversity and the importance of conservation.

The legend of the Jersey Devil can serve as a catalyst for inspiring interest in protecting the natural habitats of the Pine Barrens. By leveraging the legend's cultural significance and promoting ecotourism, conservation awareness, and research opportunities, stakeholders can work together to safeguard this ecologically rich and valuable region for future generations.

Promoting the legend of the Jersey Devil for conservation purposes can have both positive and negative ecological impacts. While the intention may be to raise awareness and protect the natural habitats of the Pine Barrens, it is essential to consider the potential consequences of using a mythical creature as a conservation tool. Here's an analysis of the potential ecological impact:

Positive Ecological Impact:

1. INCREASED AWARENESS: Promoting the legend can increase public interest in the Pine Barrens and its wildlife. This heightened awareness may lead to greater concern for the region's ecological value and foster a sense of stewardship among visitors and local communities.

2. Support for Conservation Efforts: Interest in the legend can attract visitors and generate revenue through ecotourism, providing financial support for conservation initiatives. The funds generated could be invested in habitat restoration, research, and conservation education.

3. Habitat Protection: With increased awareness and public interest, there may be greater political will and community support for protecting the Pine Barrens' habitats from development, logging, and other threats.

Negative Ecological Impact:

1. DISTURBANCE TO WILDLIFE: Increased human activity associated with legend-based tourism, such as hiking, camping, and guided tours, can lead to disturbance of wildlife and their habitats. Animals may alter their behavior or abandon nesting sites in response to human presence.

2. Habitat Degradation: Unplanned or unregulated ecotourism can lead to habitat degradation, particularly in sensitive areas. Trampling, littering, and habitat fragmentation can harm the Pine Barrens' delicate ecosystems.

3. Introduction of Invasive Species: Uncontrolled tourism and visitation can inadvertently introduce invasive species into the region. These species can disrupt the existing ecological balance and negatively impact native flora and fauna.

4. Misinterpretation of Conservation Goals: Using a mythical creature for conservation purposes may lead to misconceptions about the region's conservation needs. Visitors may focus more

on the legend than on the actual ecological issues threatening the Pine Barrens.

5. Sensationalism and Misinformation: Overemphasis on the mythical aspects of the legend may overshadow the true ecological importance of the Pine Barrens. Sensationalism and misinformation could lead to a lack of focus on genuine conservation priorities.

6. Habitat Fragmentation: Increased tourism and development associated with the legend may lead to habitat fragmentation, isolating populations of wildlife and reducing genetic diversity.

To mitigate potential negative impacts, it is crucial to implement responsible and sustainable tourism practices. Conservation efforts should be grounded in scientific research and guided by ecological data rather than solely relying on the promotion of a mythical creature. Collaboration between conservation organizations, researchers, and local communities is essential to strike a balance between promoting the legend for awareness and protecting the ecological integrity of the Pine Barrens.

Chapter 16: Skeptics and Debunkers

Skeptics and debunkers who reject the existence of the Jersey Devil put forth several arguments based on scientific reasoning, historical context, and logical analysis. Their perspectives challenge the authenticity of the legend and highlight potential explanations for the sightings and reports. Here are some common arguments put forth by skeptics:

1. Lack of Physical Evidence: One of the primary arguments against the existence of the Jersey Devil is the absence of tangible physical evidence. Despite numerous reported sightings and alleged findings, no verified remains, specimens, or conclusive evidence have ever been produced to substantiate the existence of the creature.

2. Misidentifications and Hoaxes: Skeptics argue that many sightings of the Jersey Devil can be attributed to misidentifications of known animals or natural phenomena. They suggest that people may have seen ordinary wildlife like owls, bats, or deer and misinterpreted them as the legendary creature. Additionally, hoaxes and pranks perpetuated by individuals seeking attention or amusement have been well-documented and can contribute to the legend's perpetuation.

3. Folklore and Urban Legends: Critics highlight that the legend of the Jersey Devil has deep roots in folklore and urban legends. They view the story as a product of cultural

storytelling and exaggeration over time, rather than a genuine account of a real creature.

4. Psychological and Sociological Factors: Skeptics point out that belief in mythical creatures like the Jersey Devil can be influenced by psychological and sociological factors. The power of suggestion, the desire to belong to a community with shared beliefs, and the influence of media and popular culture can contribute to the spread of the legend.

5. Historical Context and Political Satire: Some skeptics argue that the Jersey Devil legend may have originated as a form of political satire or social commentary. Historical events and political rivalries could have been intertwined with the legend to make a point or entertain the public.

6. Lack of Consistency in Descriptions: The descriptions of the Jersey Devil vary widely across different accounts, with no standardized or consistent features attributed to the creature. This lack of consistency raises questions about the creature's actual existence.

7. No Verified Sightings: Despite many claims of sightings, no verified and scientifically documented encounters with the Jersey Devil have been reported. Skeptics contend that the absence of reliable and credible eyewitness accounts further weakens the case for its existence.

Skeptics and debunkers who reject the existence of the Jersey Devil raise valid points grounded in empirical evidence and scientific inquiry. They challenge the credibility of the legend by highlighting the lack of physical evidence, the influence of folklore and urban legends, and the potential for misidentifications and hoaxes. While the Jersey Devil remains a captivating and enduring part of American folklore, the absence of verifiable evidence remains a key consideration in evaluating its existence.

Skeptics and debunkers who counter the claims of sightings and encounters of the Jersey Devil provide several types of evidence to challenge the authenticity of these accounts. Their analysis often focuses on rational explanations, scientific reasoning, and critical evaluation of the reported evidence. Here are some key points skeptics use to challenge the claims:

1. Misidentifications of Known Animals: Skeptics argue that many sightings of the Jersey Devil can be attributed to misidentifications of common animals found in the Pine Barrens and surrounding areas. For example, large owls or birds of prey flying at a distance might appear eerie or unfamiliar, leading to mistaken associations with the legendary creature's description.

2. Hoaxes and Pranks: Skeptics point out the historical prevalence of hoaxes and pranks related to the Jersey Devil. Individuals seeking attention or amusement have staged sightings or created fake evidence, leading to a proliferation of misleading accounts that add to the legend's mystery.

3. Lack of Consistency in Descriptions: The accounts of the Jersey Devil vary significantly, with descriptions ranging from a horse-like creature with wings to more humanoid figures. Skeptics argue that the lack of consistency in these accounts

raises questions about the creature's true appearance and existence.

4. Absence of Physical Evidence: The absence of tangible physical evidence, such as remains, DNA samples, or verified photographs, is a critical point made by skeptics. Despite numerous reported sightings, no conclusive evidence supporting the existence of the Jersey Devil has ever been produced.

5. Influence of Folklore and Urban Legends: Skeptics emphasize that the legend of the Jersey Devil has deep roots in folklore and urban legends, and many sightings may be influenced by these cultural narratives. The power of suggestion and shared beliefs within communities can perpetuate the legend and lead people to interpret phenomena through the lens of the folklore.

6. Psychological and Sociological Factors: Skeptics consider psychological and sociological factors that can contribute to the spread of the legend. The desire to belong to a community with shared beliefs, the influence of media and popular culture, and the propensity for sensationalism can shape how sightings and encounters are perceived and reported.

7. No Verified and Documented Sightings: Despite numerous claims of sightings and encounters, skeptics argue that no scientifically verified and documented encounters with the Jersey Devil have been reported. Without reliable and credible eyewitness accounts, the credibility of the legend is further called into question.

HAUNTED BY THE JERSEY DEVIL: A JOURNEY INTO AMERICAN FOLKLORE

Skeptics present compelling evidence and arguments to counter the claims of sightings and encounters of the Jersey Devil. Their analysis often emphasizes rational explanations, the influence of folklore and urban legends, and the lack of concrete physical evidence. While the legend remains a captivating part of American folklore, the skepticism surrounding its existence underscores the importance of critical thinking, empirical evidence, and scientific inquiry in evaluating extraordinary claims.

The dynamics between believers and skeptics regarding the legend of the Jersey Devil play a crucial role in the perpetuation and evolution of the legend over time. These two groups often hold contrasting viewpoints and engage in ongoing debates, which can have significant implications for how the legend is perceived and shared. Let's examine the dynamics between believers and skeptics and their implications:

1. Polarization and Confirmation Bias: The opposing views of believers and skeptics can lead to polarization within communities interested in the legend. Believers may be more inclined to accept and propagate stories and evidence that support the existence of the Jersey Devil, while skeptics tend to be more critical and dismissive of such claims. This polarization can reinforce confirmation bias, where individuals seek out information that aligns with their preexisting beliefs, further perpetuating the legend within their respective circles.

2. Strengthening of Belief Systems: For believers, the existence of skeptics may strengthen their conviction in the legend's authenticity. The perception of being challenged or confronted

by skeptics may reinforce their commitment to the belief and make the legend an integral part of their cultural identity.

3. Legend as a Cultural Tradition: The ongoing dialogue between believers and skeptics contributes to the legend's status as a cultural tradition. The debate becomes part of the folklore itself, enriching the narrative and keeping the legend alive through generations.

4. Media and Pop Culture Influence: The clash between believers and skeptics often attracts media attention and fuels pop culture portrayals of the Jersey Devil. Movies, TV shows, books, and internet discussions often draw on the tension between belief and skepticism, further popularizing the legend and enhancing its mystique.

5. Impacts on Local Communities: In regions where the Jersey Devil legend holds cultural significance, the dynamics between believers and skeptics can have social implications. The legend can serve as a rallying point for community identity and pride, while skepticism may be seen as challenging or dismissing local traditions.

6. Conservation and Tourism: The legend's perpetuation can have economic and environmental implications. On one hand, the promotion of the legend through tourism can boost local economies by attracting visitors. On the other hand, it may lead to potential challenges related to sustainable tourism and conservation efforts if not carefully managed.

7. Evolution and Adaptation: The ongoing debate between believers and skeptics also influences how the legend evolves

over time. It may lead to variations and adaptations of the story, accommodating new cultural, political, and social contexts while retaining its core elements.

The dynamics between believers and skeptics regarding the legend of the Jersey Devil are essential factors shaping its perpetuation and cultural significance. The clash of viewpoints influences how the legend is passed down through generations, affects local communities, and plays a role in popular media representations. While belief and skepticism create a dynamic narrative around the legend, it is essential to approach the topic with an open mind, critical thinking, and an appreciation for its cultural and historical context.

Chapter 17: The Legacy of the Jersey Devil

The enduring legacy of the Jersey Devil extends beyond the borders of New Jersey, making it one of the most famous and iconic folktales in American culture. The legend has left a profound impact on various aspects of society, ranging from tourism and popular culture to folklore and regional identity. Let's reflect on the enduring legacy of the Jersey Devil:

1. Cultural Symbol: The Jersey Devil has become a significant cultural symbol representing the folklore and heritage of New Jersey. It is an integral part of the state's identity and remains a popular subject of storytelling and local traditions.

2. Tourist Attraction: The legend of the Jersey Devil has transformed the Pine Barrens region into a hub for cryptotourism and ecotourism. Visitors from around the world are drawn to the area in hopes of encountering the mythical creature, driving local economies through the tourism industry.

3. Popular Culture: The Jersey Devil has become an enduring figure in popular culture, featuring prominently in literature, films, television shows, and video games. Countless books and movies have been inspired by the legend, further perpetuating its presence in contemporary entertainment.

4. Folklore and Storytelling: The tale of the Jersey Devil continues to be passed down through generations as a part

of American folklore. Families, communities, and local groups keep the legend alive through storytelling, enriching the narrative with their own interpretations.

5. Legacy of Mystery: The enduring legacy of the Jersey Devil lies in its ability to maintain an air of mystery and uncertainty. The lack of concrete evidence regarding its existence keeps the legend shrouded in intrigue, allowing it to captivate imaginations and spark debates between believers and skeptics.

6. Identity and Regional Pride: The legend of the Jersey Devil has contributed to a sense of regional pride among New Jersey residents. It serves as a unique aspect of the state's history, with many locals embracing the folklore as part of their cultural identity.

7. Environmental Conservation: The legend's association with the Pine Barrens has inadvertently brought attention to the ecological importance of the region. While the legend itself may be fictional, it has raised awareness about the need to protect the natural habitats of the area.

8. Internet and Social Media Impact: In the digital age, the Jersey Devil's legacy has been further amplified through the internet and social media. Online forums, websites, and social media platforms facilitate discussions, sightings reports, and speculation about the creature, keeping the legend alive in the digital landscape.

The enduring legacy of the Jersey Devil in New Jersey and beyond is a testament to the power of folklore, storytelling, and cultural symbols. The tale of the Jersey Devil continues to captivate the public imagination, leaving an indelible mark on American folklore, popular culture, and regional identity. Whether through tourism, literature, or online discussions, the legend of the Jersey Devil remains an iconic part of American folklore, weaving itself into the fabric of society and leaving an enduring impression on generations to come.

The legend of the Jersey Devil has had a profound impact on shaping local identity and folklore traditions in the regions surrounding the Pine Barrens of New Jersey. It has become an integral part of the cultural heritage of the area, influencing various aspects of local identity and storytelling practices. Here's how the legend has shaped local identity and folklore traditions:

1. Cultural Symbol and Regional Icon: The Jersey Devil has become a cultural symbol and regional icon, representing the unique folklore and history of New Jersey. It is often used as a recognizable emblem on merchandise, logos, and tourism materials, reinforcing its significance in the local identity.

2. Community Bonding: The legend fosters a sense of community bonding among residents of the Pine Barrens and nearby regions. Local residents often share stories and anecdotes about the creature, strengthening their ties to the area and reinforcing their shared identity as part of the legend's lore.

3. Storytelling and Oral Tradition: The tale of the Jersey Devil has become a central element of local storytelling and oral tradition. Families, friends, and communities pass down the

legend through generations, preserving the folklore and enriching the narrative with each retelling.

4. Local Festivals and Events: The legend has inspired various festivals and events in the region, celebrating the folklore and embracing the legend's cultural significance. These gatherings provide opportunities for locals to come together, share stories, and revel in their shared identity.

5. Naming of Landmarks and Businesses: The legend's influence is evident in the naming of landmarks, businesses, and establishments in the area. Hotels, restaurants, and shops often incorporate references to the Jersey Devil, reflecting its impact on local identity and tourism.

6. Folk Art and Crafts: The Jersey Devil legend has inspired various forms of folk art and crafts, such as paintings, sculptures, and crafts depicting the mythical creature. Local artists and artisans contribute to the preservation and continuation of the legend's presence in the region.

7. Regional Pride: The legend has instilled a sense of regional pride among New Jersey residents. The belief in the folklore and the identification with the story creates a unique bond between locals and their cultural heritage.

8. Incorporation in Education: The Jersey Devil legend is sometimes incorporated into local school curricula as part of cultural and historical studies. This inclusion helps ensure that the legend remains a part of the region's identity for future generations.

9. Connection to Natural Heritage: The legend's association with the Pine Barrens underscores the region's natural heritage and ecological significance. It has contributed to a deeper appreciation for the unique ecosystems found in the area and the importance of their preservation.

The legend of the Jersey Devil has become an inseparable part of local identity and folklore traditions in the regions surrounding the Pine Barrens. Its cultural symbolism, storytelling practices, and impact on regional pride have contributed to its enduring presence in the collective memory of New Jersey residents. Through local festivals, storytelling events, and incorporation in education, the legend continues to shape the cultural fabric of the area, reinforcing its significance in the cultural heritage of the region.

The legend of the Jersey Devil has a long and storied history, and its future developments are likely to be influenced by various factors, including advancements in technology, changes in popular culture, and evolving storytelling practices. Here are some potential future developments in the legend and its continued influence on popular culture:

1. Evolving Pop Culture Representations: As popular culture evolves, the legend of the Jersey Devil is likely to be reimagined and incorporated into new media formats. It may find its way into virtual reality experiences, augmented reality games, or interactive storytelling platforms, allowing audiences to engage with the legend in innovative ways.

2. Social Media Impact: The digital age and social media will continue to play a significant role in perpetuating the legend. Online communities, forums, and platforms enable enthusiasts and believers to share sightings, discuss folklore, and speculate on the existence of the creature, ensuring the legend's continued presence in the digital landscape.

3. Expansion of Cryptozoology and Paranormal Investigations: The enduring popularity of the Jersey Devil legend may lead to an increase in cryptozoological and paranormal investigations in the Pine Barrens and beyond. Researchers and enthusiasts may explore the region in search of new evidence or encounters, further fueling the legend's mystique.

4. Environmental Conservation Efforts: The legend's association with the Pine Barrens and its ecological importance may prompt increased efforts in environmental conservation. Organizations and advocates could leverage the legend's appeal to promote sustainable practices and protect the unique habitats of the area.

5. Reinterpretation in Literature and Film: Writers and filmmakers will likely continue to draw inspiration from the Jersey Devil legend, reinterpreting it for contemporary audiences. New literary works, movies, and TV shows could explore different aspects of the legend and its implications for modern society.

6. Cultural Festivals and Events: Local festivals and events celebrating the Jersey Devil are likely to continue and

potentially expand. These gatherings serve as opportunities for communities to embrace their folklore, fostering a sense of regional pride and cultural identity.

7. Influence on Regional Tourism: The legend's impact on tourism is likely to persist, attracting visitors interested in exploring the Pine Barrens and experiencing the legend's cultural significance. Sustainable tourism efforts could further promote the region's natural beauty and ecological importance.

8. Inclusion in Education: The legend may continue to be included in educational curricula to teach students about cultural heritage, folklore, and critical thinking. It could serve as a case study for exploring how legends and myths shape regional identity and belief systems.

9. Cross-Cultural Exchange: As the legend's popularity extends beyond New Jersey, it may cross cultural boundaries and influence the folklore of other regions. The Jersey Devil's narrative elements could blend with other local legends, creating new hybrid folktales.

The legend of the Jersey Devil is poised to continue its influence on popular culture and folklore for the foreseeable future. As society progresses, the legend will likely adapt to new media, technological advancements, and storytelling practices while retaining its allure and mystique. Its impact on regional identity, environmental conservation, and popular culture will continue to resonate with audiences, ensuring the legend's enduring legacy for generations to come.

OLIVER LANCASTER

Conclusion

The exploration of the legend of the Jersey Devil has yielded several key findings and insights, shedding light on its historical origins, cultural impact, and enduring allure:

1. Historical Origins: The legend of the Jersey Devil can be traced back to the 18th century with various theories attributing its origins to political satire, religious beliefs, and local folklore. Over time, the tale has evolved and become an integral part of American folklore.

2. Cultural Significance: The Jersey Devil is deeply ingrained in the cultural heritage of New Jersey and beyond, serving as a symbol of regional identity and pride. It has influenced local traditions, storytelling practices, and the naming of landmarks and businesses.

3. Popular Culture: The legend's influence extends to popular culture, inspiring literature, films, TV shows, and other media representations. It continues to captivate the public imagination, ensuring its presence in contemporary entertainment.

4. Tourism and Ecotourism: The legend has transformed the Pine Barrens region into a hub for cryptotourism and ecotourism, attracting visitors from around the world. This influx of tourists contributes to local economies and fosters awareness about environmental conservation.

5. Belief and Skepticism: The legend of the Jersey Devil has sparked ongoing debates between believers and skeptics. These opposing viewpoints contribute to the perpetuation of the legend and influence its cultural significance.

6. Environmental Conservation: While the Jersey Devil may be fictional, its association with the Pine Barrens has inadvertently drawn attention to the region's ecological importance. It has become a symbol for advocating habitat protection and sustainable practices.

7. Blurred Lines Between Fact and Fiction: The legend exemplifies how folklore and urban legends can blur the lines between fact and fiction. The absence of concrete evidence challenges the veracity of the tale, but the legend's allure persists.

8. Influence on Local Identity: The Jersey Devil has shaped the local identity of New Jersey, reinforcing a sense of community bonding and regional pride. Its inclusion in education ensures the legend remains a part of the cultural fabric for future generations.

9. Continued Perpetuation: The legend's perpetuation is facilitated by the internet and social media, allowing enthusiasts to share stories, sightings, and speculations. The legend's dynamic narrative ensures its ongoing relevance.

The legend of the Jersey Devil represents a fascinating blend of folklore, history, and cultural impact. Its enduring legacy reflects the power of storytelling and its ability to shape identities, inspire exploration, and captivate the public imagination across generations. The tale's continued influence in various aspects of society underscores its significance as a treasured piece of American folklore and a timeless source of intrigue.

The enduring allure of mythical creatures and their place in human culture can be attributed to several profound and intrinsic aspects of the human experience. Throughout history, mythical creatures have held a special fascination for people of all ages and cultures. Here are some final reflections on why these creatures continue to captivate and resonate with humanity:

1. The Power of Imagination: Mythical creatures exist beyond the boundaries of reality, allowing the human imagination to run wild. They embody the unknown and the mysterious, opening doors to realms of wonder and fantasy that spark creativity and storytelling.

2. Symbolism and Archetypes: Mythical creatures often embody powerful archetypal symbols that reflect aspects of human nature and the human psyche. They represent primal fears, desires, and aspirations, making them vehicles for exploring deep-seated emotions and concepts.

3. Cultural Identity and Belief Systems: Myths and legends featuring mythical creatures are essential components of cultural identity and belief systems. They bind communities together, shaping their values, rituals, and understanding of the world.

4. Explaining the Unexplained: In the past, mythical creatures provided explanations for natural phenomena that were beyond early human comprehension. They served as a way to make sense of the world and its mysteries.

5. Moral Lessons and Wisdom: Myths often use mythical creatures to convey moral lessons and impart wisdom. These stories teach virtues, warn against vices, and provide guidance on navigating life's challenges.

6. The Quest for Adventure: Myths featuring heroic quests and encounters with mythical creatures tap into the human desire for adventure and exploration. They offer tales of heroism, courage, and triumph over adversity.

7. Connection with Nature: Many mythical creatures are associated with the natural world and its elements. They personify nature's power and serve as a reminder of humanity's interconnectedness with the environment.

8. Continuity and Timelessness: The enduring appeal of mythical creatures lies in their timeless nature. They have been passed down through generations, adapting to different cultures while retaining their core allure.

9. Source of Comfort and Wonder: In a world often filled with uncertainties, mythical creatures offer a sense of comfort and wonder. They provide an escape from reality and transport us to magical realms where anything is possible.

Mythical creatures hold a timeless place in human culture because they resonate with fundamental aspects of the human experience. They reflect our imagination, emotions, and quest for understanding the world around us. As they continue to inspire awe, curiosity, and storytelling, mythical creatures will forever remain cherished and cherished in the human collective consciousness.

Embracing the mysteries of the world is a journey that can lead us to new horizons of wonder and discovery. As we delve into the realms of folklore, myths, and legendary creatures like the Jersey Devil, let us be inspired by the magic of the unknown while maintaining a critical and curious mind. Here's an encouragement to embrace the mysteries of the world while remaining critical thinkers and explorers:

1. Cultivate Wonder: Embrace the enchantment of mysteries, for they spark wonder and awe that ignite our imaginations. Be open to the possibility of the extraordinary, for it is in the unknown that we often find the most captivating stories and insights.

2. Embrace Diversity: The world is a tapestry of diverse cultures, each with its own myths and folklore. Appreciate the richness of these narratives and the unique perspectives they offer. Embrace the diversity of beliefs while respecting differing viewpoints.

3. Seek Knowledge: As we explore the mysteries, let us do so with a thirst for knowledge. Engage in research, seek evidence, and challenge assumptions. Critical thinking allows us to distinguish between fact and fiction, ensuring we approach legends with discernment.

4. Inspire Creativity: Myths and legends are wellsprings of creativity. Let them inspire you to tell your own tales and craft new narratives that resonate with the human experience.

5. Connect with Nature: The mythical creatures of folklore often reflect our connection with nature. Let their stories remind us of our role as stewards of the environment. Embrace the mystery and beauty of the natural world while cherishing and protecting its wonders.

6. Embrace the Journey: Life itself is a journey into the unknown. Embrace the twists and turns, for they lead us to new opportunities for growth and understanding. Approach the mysteries with a sense of adventure and curiosity.

7. Remain Open-Minded: The pursuit of knowledge requires an open mind. Embrace the mysteries, but also be willing to revise your beliefs in light of new evidence and understanding.

8. Cherish the Enchantment: The mysteries of the world provide us with a sense of enchantment and magic. Let us cherish these moments and hold on to the childlike wonder that resides within us all.

As we embrace the mysteries of the world with both a sense of wonder and critical thinking, we embark on a journey of intellectual and emotional growth. Let us be explorers of our own lives, venturing into the unknown with courage and curiosity. The mysteries we encounter may not always yield definitive answers, but the journey itself will enrich our souls and inspire us to appreciate the marvels that surround us.

Embrace the enigma, and let the pursuit of knowledge be your guiding star.

Sign up to my free newsletter to get updates on new releases, FREE teaser chapters to upcoming releases and FREE digital short stories.

Or visit https://tinyurl.com/olanc

I never spam and you can unsubscribe at any time.

Don't miss out!

Visit the website below and you can sign up to receive emails whenever Oliver Lancaster publishes a new book. There's no charge and no obligation.

https://books2read.com/r/B-A-UNEZ-WWIMC

BOOKS 2 READ

Connecting independent readers to independent writers.

Also by Oliver Lancaster

Chernobyl: Unveiling the tragedy. A Comprehensive Account of the Nuclear Disaster

The Bhopal Gas Tragedy: Unraveling the Catastrophe of 1984

The Deepwater Horizon Oil Spill of 2010: A Disaster Unveiled

Fukushima Fallout: Unveiling the Truth behind the 2011 Nuclear Disaster

Minamata Disease: Poisoned Waters and the Battle for Justice (1932-1968)

Evil Women: Unmasking History's Most Notorious Women

Bundy The Dark Chronicles: America's Infamous Serial Killer

Dahmer The Dark Chronicles: America's Infamous Milwaukee Cannibal

Zodiac The Dark Chronicles: America's Infamous Cryptic Killer

Bigfoot: The Comprehensive Investigation into the Elusive Legend

Chasing Legends: The Truth behind the Chupacabra

Chasing Legends: The Truth behind the Loch Ness Monster

Aokigahara Forest: The Heartbreaking Secrets of Japan's Suicide Forest

The Amityville House: The Haunting Secrets of America's Most Infamous Residence

The Stanley Hotel: The Mystery of Colorado's Historic Landmark

The Tower of London: The Haunted Past and Secrets of Royal Ghosts

The Winchester Mystery House: The Riddle of Sarah Winchester's Mansion

Vanished Skies: The Mysterious Disappearance of Amelia Earhart

Vanishing Point: The Bermuda Triangle Exposed

Poveglia Island: Haunting Secrets of Italy's Most Terrifying Haunted Destination

Tracing Footsteps: The Mystery of Madeleine McCann

Inferno in the Sky: The Hindenburg Disaster

Challenger: Tragedy and Triumph - Unraveling the Space Shuttle Challenger Explosion

Collision Course: Unraveling The Tenerife Airport Disaster

Haunted by the Jersey Devil: A Journey into American Folklore

Sweet Tragedy: Unraveling The Boston Molasses Disaster

Watch for more at https://tinyurl.com/olanc.

About the Author

Oliver Lancaster possesses an enchanting charm that effortlessly draws readers into the depths of his literary world. With an insatiable curiosity for the unexplained, he skillfully weaves tales of crime, conspiracy, mystery and the unknown, leaving readers on the edge of their seats.

Nestled away in the seclusion of his garden shed, Oliver finds solace and inspiration in the tranquility of nature. Surrounded by greenery and fragrant blooms, he dives into a realm of imagination, unearthing secrets that lie hidden within his mind.

Accompanying Oliver on his literary ventures is his faithful ginger cat named Italics. With his mesmerizing gaze and mysterious mannerisms, Italics adds an air of intrigue to Oliver's writing process, often curling up on a cushioned chair nearby, watching as words flow effortlessly from his human companion's pen.

When not engrossed in his craft, Oliver indulges in the gentle warmth of his garden with a glass of red wine.

Prepare to be spellbound as you delve into the pages of Oliver Lancaster's novels, for he is a master of the eerie, a weaver of secrets, and an unrivaled guide through the labyrinthine corridors of the human psyche.

Sign up to a free newsletter to get updates on new releases, FREE teaser chapters to upcoming releases and FREE digital short stories.

Read more at https://tinyurl.com/olanc.

www.ingramcontent.com/pod-product-compliance
Lightning Source LLC
Chambersburg PA
CBHW050519160726
48003CB00001B/378